DISCOVERING GOD'S
KINGDOM PURPOSE
FOR YOUR LIFE

STUDENTS ON THE RISE

SR. ACTIVATION JOURNAL

JOHNNY & ELIZABETH ENLOW

Copyright © 2024 by Johnny Enlow & Elizabeth Enlow

All rights reserved. No part of this publication may be reproduced, distributed, or transmitted in any form or by any means, including photocopying, recording, or other electronic or mechanical methods, without the prior written permission of the publisher, except in the case of brief quotations embodied in critical reviews and certain other noncommercial uses permitted by copyright law. For permission requests, write to the publisher at the address below.

Fedd Books
P.O. Box 341973
Austin, TX 78734

www.thefeddagency.com

Published in association with The Fedd Agency, Inc., a literary agency.

ISBN: 978-1-957616-81-0

LCCN: 2024937195

Printed in the United States of America

CONTENTS

CHAPTER 1: PREPARING FOR THE JOURNEY 7

CHAPTER 2: MOUNTAIN OF FAMILY 49

CHAPTER 3: MOUNTAIN OF RELIGION 89

CHAPTER 4: MOUNTAIN OF EDUCATION 129

CHAPTER 5: MOUNTAIN OF ECONOMY 169

CHAPTER 6: MOUNTAIN OF ARTS & ENTERTAINMENT 209

CHAPTER 7: MOUNTAIN OF MEDIA 249

CHAPTER 8: MOUNTAIN OF GOVERNMENT 289

CHAPTER 9: YOU ARE A GENERATION OF REFORMERS 329

In this activation journal, you will find the following components to support each of the chapters and lessons in the *Students on the RISE* curriculum. The activities, assignments, and discussions may be facilitator-led or independent study. As you journal and respond to the prompts, always remember to ask God how this particular piece of knowledge or revelation might be informing your personal journey. If He shares something, be sure to capture it for future reflection.

The **RISE Affirmation** for each lesson is a short, but powerful statement to read and believe about yourself. The enemy wants to prevent you from rising to your full potential by causing you to think less about yourself than God does. These affirming statements are meant to remind you of the truth and give you discernment to realize when and how Satan lies to you and holds you back with insecurity. Memorize these as weapons against the enemy!

The **RISE Anchor** for each lesson are verses from the Bible to equip you for your climb. Scripture is our standard for truth and one of the ways God speaks to us. You were created to hear His voice, but how will you recognize the ways He talks to you throughout your everyday life if you don't have the foundation of His original words from the Bible? Read these and apply them personally to your life. Although the Bible was written a long time ago, His words and truth remain forever and are still applicable to us today. Consider looking up each of the verses for the day and highlighting them in your Bible with the coordinating color of that mountain.

The **RISE Mountain Climber Meetup** at the end of each day's lesson is where you will learn and remember the most. It's one thing to read what someone else is teaching you, but it's much more impactful when you take the time to think about it for yourself and how you specifically relate to it. If you have another student or group you are with, this is meant to be a time of discussion with each other as fellow mountain climbers. If you are going through this as a solo climber, be sure to take time to journal your thoughts, questions, and ideas.

The **RISE Assignment** represents the last lesson or day in a chapter and is where we take a day hike up the mountain taking what you have learned and applying it to different scenarios.

PREPARING FOR THE JOURNEY

CHAPTER 1

Day 1 – Let's Go Climb a Mountain!

Day 2 – You've Been Commissioned

Day 3 – The King and His Kingdom Come Together

Day 4 – Don't Repeat History

Day 5 – The Cure for End-times-itis

Day 6 – The Mountain of the House of the Lord

Day 7 – Live On Purpose

Day 8 – The Seven Spirits of God

Day 9 – Satan's Big Lies About God

Day 10 – Our Big Truths About God

DAY 1
LET'S GO CLIMB A MOUNTAIN

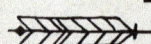 **ESSENTIAL #1**

A reformer must understand the Seven Mountain Mandate: Fill the earth with the knowledge of the glory of God.

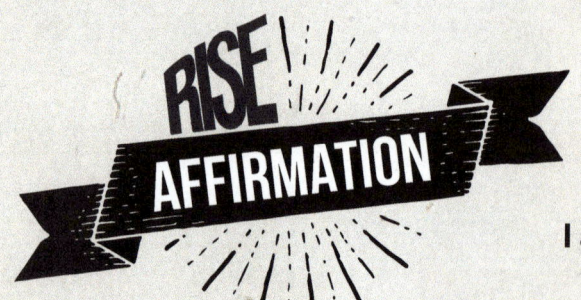

I am a MEGA-REFormer.

Revelation 4:5 (NKJV) — "From the throne proceeded lightnings, thunderings, and voices. Seven lamps of fire *were* burning before the throne, which are the seven Spirits of God."

Habakkuk 2:14, Isaiah 11:9 (NKJV) — "The knowledge of the glory of God will cover the Earth..."

Romans 8:18-21 (NKJV) — "For I consider that the sufferings of this present time are not worthy *to be compared* with the glory which shall be revealed in us. For the earnest expectation of the creation eagerly waits for the revealing of the sons of God. For the creation was subjected to futility, not willingly, but because of Him who subjected *it* in hope; because the creation itself also will be delivered from the bondage of corruption into the glorious liberty of the children of God."

Now that you've learned what it means to be a reformer and what the Seven Mountain Mandate means, take some time to consider the discussion questions below.

1. What are three recommendations you would give to a friend seeking God regarding their influence or impact in the Kingdom?

2. As you think about the mountain you're most drawn to, try to identify three problems you've seen or experienced on that mountain.

3. Dream with God and imagine how you could bring solutions to one or more of these areas on your mountain of influence. What impact will your solution have?

DAY 2
YOU'VE BEEN COMMISSIONED

 **ESSENTIAL #2**

A reformer must understand how authority over the Seven Mountains was lost and regained.

I am commissioned.

Matthew 18:11 (NKJV) — "The Son of Man came to save that which was lost."

Matthew 28:18-19 (NKJV) — "All authority has been given to Me in Heaven and on Earth. Go therefore and make disciples of all nations."

1 Timothy 2:5-6 (NKJV) — "For *there is* one God and one mediator between God and men, *the* Man Christ Jesus, who gave himself as a ransom for all, to be testified in due time."

Now that you understand how the authority over the Seven Mountains of culture was lost and how it can be regained, take some time to reflect with the Holy Spirit or discuss with a leader or small group on what the authority you've been given truly means.

1. Consider and write down some of the thoughts or questions that come up as you think about the knowledge (awareness) of the glory of the Lord covering the Earth—through you! How could that happen?

2. What do you think the glory of God filling the earth will look like through your life story and the good things you do that God planned for you?

3. Share the impact of realizing that your story is part of God's glory filling the earth. Have you ever thought about this? Does this realization motivate you?

DAY 3
THE KING AND HIS KINGDOM COME TOGETHER

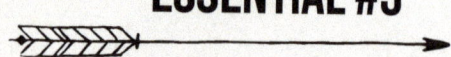
ESSENTIAL #3

A reformer must understand the Gospel of the Kingdom vs. the Gospel of Salvation.

I am a believer in Jesus.

John 3:16 (NIV) — "For God loved the world so much that He gave His one and only Son, so that everyone who believes in Him will not perish but have eternal life."

Matthew 24:14 (NKJV) — "And this gospel of the kingdom will be preached in all the world as a witness to all the nations, and then the end will come."

Romans 10: 16-18 (NKJV) — "But they have not all obeyed the gospel. For Isaiah says, 'Lord, who has believed our report?' So, then faith *comes* by hearing, and hearing by the word of God. But I say, have they not heard? Yes indeed: 'Their sound has gone out to all the earth, and their words to the ends of the world.'"

Now that you understand the difference between the Gospel of the Kingdom and the Gospel of Salvation, reflect on the discussion questions below with the Holy Spirit or discuss with a leader or small group to think about these differences and the effect they can have as we share the good news of God's Kingdom.

1. Share your experience of choosing God's gift of redemption.

2. Describe the difference between the Gospel of the Kingdom and the Gospel of Salvation in your own words.

3. What are some strategies to ensure that you're sharing the Gospel of the Kingdom rather than just the Gospel of Salvation with others?

DAY 4
DON'T REPEAT HISTORY

 **ESSENTIAL #4** A reformer must understand influence vs. dominionism.

 I am an influencer.

 **Genesis 1:26, 28** (NKJV) — "God said, 'Let us make man in Our image, according to Our likeness; let them have dominion over the fish of the sea, over the birds of the air, over the cattle, over all the earth and over every creeping thing that creeps on the earth'...Then

God blessed them and said to them, 'Be fruitful and multiply; fill the earth and subdue it; have dominion over the fish of the sea, the birds of the air, and over every living things that moves on earth.'"

Ephesians 6:12 (NKJV) — "We do not wrestle against flesh and blood (people), but against principalities, against powers, against the rulers of the darkness of this age (Satan and his demons)…"

Ephesians 2:10 (NKJV) — "For we are his workmanship, created in Christ Jesus for good works, which God prepared beforehand, that we should walk in them."

Now that we've covered the difference between influence and imposition or domination, take some time to reflect on the prompts below with the Holy Spirit or discuss with a leader or small group. Remember, we want to be influencers for God!

1. Have you ever tried to get someone to agree with you using force or manipulative tactics? Or has someone ever done that to you? Describe the situation. How did it leave you feeling? How could it have been different?

2. How do you know when the enemy is attempting to work through you?

DAY 5
THE CURE FOR END-TIMES-ITIS

ESSENTIAL #5

A reformer must understand the end-times narrative and have value for our planet.

I am a part of the correct narrative.

Acts 3:21 (NLT) — "For He (Jesus) must remain in Heaven until the time for the final restoration of all things, as God promised long ago through His holy prophets."

Matthew 13:41, 43a (NLT) — "The Son of Man will send his angels, and they will remove from His Kingdom everything that causes sin and all who do evil...Then the righteous will shine like the sun in their Father's Kingdom."

Ezekiel 36:25-27 (NKJV) — "Then I will sprinkle clean water on you, and you shall be clean; I will cleanse you from all your filthiness and from all your idols. I will give you a new heart and put a new spirit within you; I will take your heart of stone out of your flesh and give you a heart of flesh. I will put My Spirit within you and cause you to walk in my statutes, and you will keep my judgements and do *them*."

Now that we've discussed the end-times narrative and the importance of taking care of the Earth, take some time to reflect on how the different end-times narratives can impact Christians and the way we walk through the world. Discuss the following prompts with a leader, small group, or use these prompts for personal reflection with the Holy Spirit.

1. Before reading this chapter, where you familiar with the concept of the "end-times"?

2. If so, how did it affect the way you thought about your role in the Kingdom of God?

3. Bigger than any superhero, Jesus saved and is in the process of saving the world. You are a part of His team. How does knowing that God's Kingdom is to be established on Earth make you feel about your active role in seeing it come to pass?

DAY 6
THE MOUNTAIN OF THE HOUSE OF THE LORD

ESSENTIAL #6

A reformer must understand the role of the church on the Seven Mountains.

I am the church.

Matthew 16:18b (ESV) — Jesus said, "...I will build My church and the gates of hell will not prevail against it."

Micah 4:1-2 (NKJV) — "Now it shall come to pass in the latter days That the mountain of the LORD's house Shall be established on the top of the mountains. And shall be exalted above the hills; And peoples shall flow to it."

Ephesians 2:22 (ESV) — "In him you are being built together into a dwelling place for God by the Spirit."

Now that you understand the true meaning and God's intention of what the church should be, take some time to reflect on the prompts below with the Holy Spirit, with a leader, or with a small group.

1. Describe how you can be the church outside the four walls of the traditional church. Give some examples that fall into each of the Seven Mountains.

2. How is your daily life a representation of the church, the body of Christ, and a reformer on a mountain of influence?

DAY 7
LIVE ON PURPOSE

 **ESSENTIAL #7**

A reformer must learn to live intentionally every day to know God, make Him known, learn to love Him, and learn how to be loved by Him.

I am intentional.

1 John 5:20 (NLT) — "And we know that the Son of God has come, and he has given us understanding so that we can know the true God. And now we live in fellowship with the true God because we live in fellowship with his Son, Jesus Christ. He is the only true God, and He is eternal life."

1 John 4:8, 19 (NLT) — "But anyone who does not love does not know God, for God is love….We love each other because He loved us first."

Colossians 1:13 (ESV) — "He has delivered us from the domain of darkness and transferred us to the kingdom of his beloved Son."

We've talked about living intentionally, seeking your purpose in Him, and learning to accept God's love and then give that love to others. Take some personal time to reflect on the questions below with the Holy Spirit, with a leader, or with a small group.

1. Do you understand that the God who created the Universe and sent His best gift as a ransom for your soul lives inside of you? If so, explain. If not, what might be some reasons for the sense of separation?

2. What are some exercises in intentionality that can help you become more aware of the reality of your oneness in Christ?

DAY 8
THE SEVEN SPIRITS OF GOD

ESSENTIAL #8

A reformer must understand that there are multiple faces, or spirits, of God.

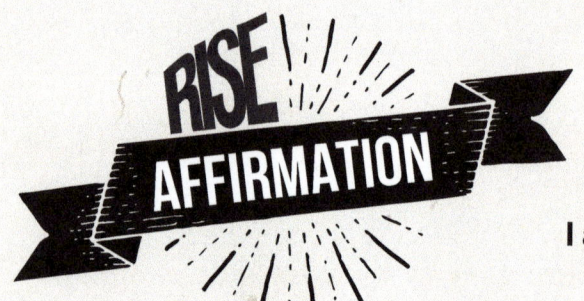

I am created to know the faces of God.

Revelation 4:5 (NKJV) — "And from the throne proceeded lightnings, thunderings, and voices. Seven lamps of fire *were* burning before the throne, which are the seven Spirits of God."

Revelation 5:6 (NLT) — "Then I saw a Lamb that looked as if it had been slaughtered...He had seven horns and seven eyes, which represent the sevenfold Spirit of God that is sent out into every part of the earth."

Zechariah 4:10 (NKJV) — "For who has despised the day of small things? For these seven rejoice to see the plumb line in the hand of Zerubbabel. They are the eyes of the Lord, which scan to and fro throughout the whole earth.'"

We've introduced you to the knowledge that God is one, three, and seven and we will unpack the seven faces of God as we move through this study. Take some time for personal reflection on the prompts below with the Holy Spirit, with a leader, or with a small group.

1. How does understanding the different faces of God help you understand and relate to Him on a more personal level as you experience different situations in your life?

2. Understanding the face of God in each of the separate Mountains of Culture is important in order to understand who God is and what He's like. Spend some time writing out how you see God on the Seven Mountains of culture currently and what truth you believe we're meant to communicate on each mountain.

DAY 9
SATAN'S BIG LIES ABOUT GOD

 **ESSENTIAL #9** A reformer must understand that our broken culture promotes lies from Satan about God.

 I am called to become an expert on God.

 **John 10:10** (NLT) — "The thief's purpose is to steal and kill and destroy. My purpose is to give them a rich and satisfying life."

John 8:32 (NLT) — "And you will know the truth, and the truth will set you free."

Galatians 5:1 (NKJV) — "Stand fast therefore in the liberty by which Christ has made us free, and do not be entangled again with a yoke of bondage."

Now that we've discussed Satan, the lies he tries to spread about God on the Seven Mountains of culture, and how it affects us and our society, take some time for personal reflection with the Holy Spirit or discuss with a leader or small group.

1. Imagine Satan's outcome of being cast down from Heaven as described in Scripture—Heaven's first screenplay. What must the exchange have been like? What might have been some of the reactions of the other Heavenly beings who were witnessing?

2. What are some ways the enemy might attempt to create lack and destruction in your life?

3. Do you think you underestimate the enemy at times? Why?

DAY 10
OUR BIG TRUTHS ABOUT GOD

ESSENTIAL #10

A reformer must understand how we overcome the lies about God in society by living the truth in the Seven Mountains.

I am bringing truth to the Seven Mountains.

2 Corinthians 10:4-5a (NKJV) — "For the weapons of our warfare are not carnal but mighty in God for pulling down strongholds, casting down arguments and every high thing that exalts itself against the knowledge of God."

1 Kings 18:39 (NKJV) — "Now when all the people saw it, they fell on their faces; and they said, 'The Lord, He is God! The Lord, He is God!'"

Philippians 4:13 (NKJV) — "I can do all things through Christ who strengthens me."

Are you ready to learn about the seven faces of God on the Seven Mountains of Culture? Now that we've covered how we can overcome Satan's lies about God on the Seven Mountains of Culture, take some time to personally reflect on the following prompts with the Holy Spirit or discuss with a leader or small group.

1. On which mountains of culture have you experienced the most lies about God? Give specific examples.

2. What truth was stolen from you that you are asking God to restore to your heart?

3. On which Mountains of Culture have you experienced the most truth about God? Give specific examples.

4. What are some ways you have helped or could help others experience that same truth?

MOUNTAIN OF FAMILY

CHAPTER 2

CHECK YOUR SUPPLIES

    Day 1 – The Face of God on the Mountain of Family

    Day 2 – The Lie About God on the Mountain of Family

    Day 3 – The Truth About God on the Mountain of Family

BASECAMP ACTIVATIONS

    Day 4 – Keep Your Two Cents

    Day 5 – Channel of Blessing

    Day 6 – Pursue Healing

    Day 7 – Remove Yourself as Judge

    Day 8 – Heirs with Jesus

    Day 9 – Love with a Pure Heart

MOUNTAIN CLIMB

    Day 10 – Day Hike on the Mountain of Family

DAY 1
THE FACE OF GOD ON THE MOUNTAIN OF FAMILY

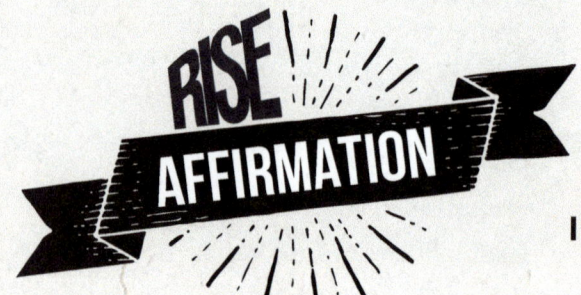

I am strong like my Papa.

Romans 8:15 (NLT) — "So you have not received a spirit that makes you fearful slaves. Instead, you received God's Spirit when He adopted you as His own children. Now we call Him, ' Abba, Father.'"

Zechariah 2:8 (NLT) — "After a period of glory, the Lord of Heaven's Armies sent me against the nations who plundered you. For He said, 'Anyone who harms you harms My most precious possession.'"

Deuteronomy 31:6 (NKJV) — "Be strong and of good courage, do not fear nor be afraid of them; for the Lord your God, He is the One who goes with you. He will not leave you nor forsake you."

Psalms 28:7 (NKJV) — "The Lord is my strength and my shield; my heart trusted in him, and I am helped; Therefore, my heart greatly rejoices, and with my song I will praise him."

Now that you've learned about the face of God on the Mountain of Family as Father and displayed as STRENGTH, take time to personally reflect on the prompts below with the Holy Spirit or with a leader or small group.

1. What are some of the lies that the enemy has told you to separate you from knowing the love of God?

2. If one lie stands out, can you identify when you began believing the lie or where it came from?

3. How could acknowledging the truth of your worth change the way you interact with people?

4. Considering that the enemy is out to counter the truth of God in your life, take the lies that you believe and ask God to help you discern the truth hidden within that the enemy is fighting so hard to keep you from. What are those truths?

DAY 2

THE LIE ABOUT GOD ON THE MOUNTAIN OF FAMILY

I am not rejected or abandoned by my Heavenly Father.

Zephaniah 3:17 (NLT) — "For the Lord your God is living among you. He is a mighty Savior. He will take delight in you with gladness. With his love, he will calm all your fears. He will rejoice over you with joyful songs."

Ephesians 6:10-11 (NLT) — "A final word: Be strong in the Lord and in His mighty power. Put on all of God's armor so that you will be able to stand firm against all strategies of the devil."

Isaiah 40:31 (NKJV) — "But those who wait on the Lord shall renew their strength; they shall mount up with wings like eagles, they shall run and not be weary, they shall walk and not faint."

Now that you understand the lie about God on the Mountain of Family and how to stand firm against Satan's strategies, below are prompts that you can use for personal reflection with the Holy Spirit or discuss with a leader or small group.

1. If you identified the lie that God has rejected and abandoned you, ask for forgiveness for believing it and break agreement with the enemy. If there are people in your family you need to forgive or make amends with, make sure to do so. Remember, an enemy exposed is an enemy defeated.

2. Identify times when you have believed a lie about God and a lie about yourself.

3. How did you come to recognize that it was a lie?

DAY 3
THE TRUTH ABOUT GOD ON THE MOUNTAIN OF FAMILY

I am accepted by my Heavenly Father.

Psalms 27:10 (NLT) — "Even if my father and mother abandon me, the LORD will hold me close."

Deuteronomy 31:6 (NLT) — "So be strong and courageous! Do not be afraid and do not panic before them. For the Lord your God will personally go ahead of you. He will neither fail you nor abandon you."

Isaiah 41:10 (NKJV) — "Fear not, for I am with you; be not dismayed, for I am your God; I will strengthen you, I will help you, I will uphold you with my righteous right hand."

Now that we've established the Truth of God on the Mountain of Family, below are questions you can use for personal reflection with the Holy Spirit or discuss with a leader or small group. Understanding the truth of your acceptance and God's love is an important steppingstone to begin climbing this mountain.

1. Reflect on God's promise in Psalms 27:10 to help get you through tough times. What confidence does it give you to know that God has your back regardless of who may let you down?

2. Write a note to your Heavenly Father to let Him know what that means to you.

3. Describe a time where you were in a tough situation. What reassurance did you have that God was there?

4. Close your eyes and picture Jesus with you in that situation. Where can you see evidence of Him in that memory?

5. What do you imagine He was feeling about you at that time?

DAY 4
KEEP YOUR TWO CENTS

You don't always have to talk about your faith to show your faith (because when you show it, then they want to know it).

I am able to keep my opinions to myself.

Ephesians 4:15 (NLT) — "Instead, we will speak the truth in love, growing in every way more and more like Christ, who is the head of His body, the church."

Philippians 4:8 (NLT) — "And now, dear brothers and sisters, one final thing. Fix your thoughts on what is true, and honorable, and right, and pure, and lovely, and admirable. Think about things that are excellent and worthy of praise."

Micah 6:8 (NKJV) — "He has shown you, O man, what is good; And what does the Lord require of you but to act justly, to love mercy, and to walk humbly with your God?"

Now that we've discussed one way to show God's love on the Mountain of Family and how you don't always have to talk about your faith to show your faith, below are prompts that you can use for personal reflection with the Holy Spirit or discuss with a leader or small group.

1. How can asking questions be a great strategy for communicating with others and leading them into asking of God for themselves?

2. How might this promote growth and understanding?

3. Do you inquire of God or do you feel those around you have attempted to give you all the answers?

4. What does it mean to call someone up instead of calling them out?

5. If you have ever been called out, how did it make you feel? How can we approach others with love and respect?

DAY 5
CHANNEL OF BLESSING

UNDERSTANDING

You can be a channel through which God's love flows.

AFFIRMATION

I am a channel of God's love.

ANCHOR

Luke 6:31 (NLT) — "Do to others as you would like them to do to you."

1 Peter 4:8 (NLT) — "Most important of all, continue to show deep love for each other, for love covers a multitude of sins."

Luke 6:35-36 (NKJV) — "But love your enemies, do good, and lend, hoping for nothing in return; and your reward will be great, and you will be sons of the Most High. For He is kind to the unthankful and evil. Therefore, be merciful, just as your Father is also merciful."

We've covered letting God's love flow through us and coming with an opposing spirit to help others see and experience God's love. Now, below are prompts that you can use for personal reflection with the Holy Spirit or discuss with a leader or small group.

1. Why does it seem easier to tell people what they are doing wrong or where they messed up rather than loving them through what can feel messy and uncomfortable?

2. In a world filled with opportunities for hurt and offense, how can we face challenges and be a source of God's love?

3. How might this promote peace and understanding, especially within our own families?

DAY 6
PURSUE HEALING

You must pursue healing of your own rejection and wounds to become a carrier of healing for others.

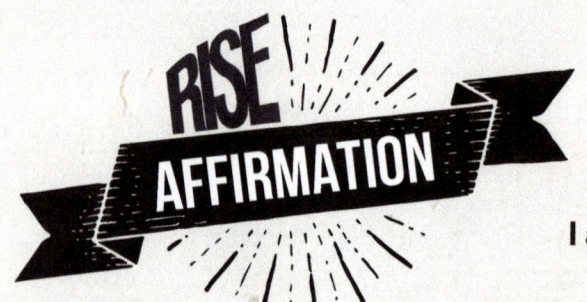

I am a healer of brokenness.

Romans 5:8 (NLT) — "But God showed His great love for us by sending Christ to die for us while we were still sinners."

2 Corinthians 3:5 (NLT) — **"**It is not that we think we are qualified to do anything on our own. Our qualification comes from God."

Psalms 34:18 (ESV) — "The Lord is near to the brokenhearted and saves the crushed in spirit."

Today, we talked about pursuing healing in your own life and family to become a carrier of healing for others and how to combat Satan's lies of rejection. Now, spend some time looking at the prompts below and use them for personal reflection with the Holy Spirit or discuss with a leader or small group.

1. When the enemy tries to convince us that we don't have what it takes, how can we respond with confidence?

2. How can we find peace and assurance in the face of fear and uncertainty?

3. What does it mean for God to be your dwelling place as described in Psalms 91?

4. Consider a time when you felt hurt or pain emotionally. What did you do?

5. How did you or could you have invited Jesus into your pain and hurt to experience healing?

6. How can you share this healing with others?

DAY 7
REMOVE YOURSELF AS JUDGE

UNDERSTANDING

You are called to display God's acceptance to everyone you meet.

AFFIRMATION

I am not a judge of others.

ANCHOR

Matthew 7:1-3 (NLT) — "Do not judge others, and you will not be judged. For you will be treated as you treat others. The standard you use in judging is the standard by which you will be judged. 'And why worry about a speck in your friend's eye when you have a log in your own?'"

James 2:13 (NLT) — "There will be no mercy for those who have not shown mercy to others. But if you have been merciful, God will be merciful when He judges you."

Colossians 3:12-14 (NKJV) — "Therefore, as the elect of God, holy and beloved, put on tender mercies, kindness, humility, meekness, longsuffering; bearing with one another, and forgiving one another, if anyone has a complaint against another; even as Christ forgave you, so you also must do. But above all these things put on love, which is the bond of perfection."

Now that we've talked about removing ourselves as a judge for others in order to be an example of God's acceptance of everyone, spend some time on the discussion questions below that you can use for personal reflection with the Holy Spirit or discuss with a leader or small group.

1. Read the Parable of the Unforgiving Debtor in Matthew 18:21-35. Compare this with the two Scriptures from the lesson and elaborate on your understanding.

2. In what ways does judgment hinder love and acceptance?

3. Have you ever felt judged? How did it make you feel?

4. How does realizing and believing that we are all made in God's image impact our understanding of His commitment to the restoration of all things?

DAY 8
HEIRS WITH JESUS

As a son or daughter of King Jesus, you are a royal heir.

I am an heir with Jesus.

Galatians 4:6-7 (NLT) — "And because we are His children, God has sent the Spirit of His Son into our hearts, prompting us to call out, "Abba, Father." Now you are no longer a slave but God's own child. And since you are His child, God has made you, His heir."

Ephesians 2:6 (NLT) — "For He raised us from the dead along with Christ and seated us with Him in the Heavenly realms because we are united with Christ Jesus."

John 1:12-13 (ESV) — "But to all who did receive him, who believed in his name, he gave the right to become children of God, who were born, not of blood nor of the will of the flesh nor of the will of man, but of God."

Today, we talked about what it means to be a child of God and the blessing and provision that comes from the knowledge. Now, below are questions that you can use for personal reflection with the Holy Spirit or discuss with a leader or small group.

1. How does the relationship with God as our Father affect our understanding of our own identity and the inheritance we've been given?

2. Is it difficult for you to know God as Father? If so, why might that be?

3. What does it mean to be seated with Christ in Heavenly places?

4. How does this position of authority and access to God's blessings impact your daily lives?

DAY 9
LOVE WITH A PURE HEART

You can model how Jesus was as a friend of sinners.

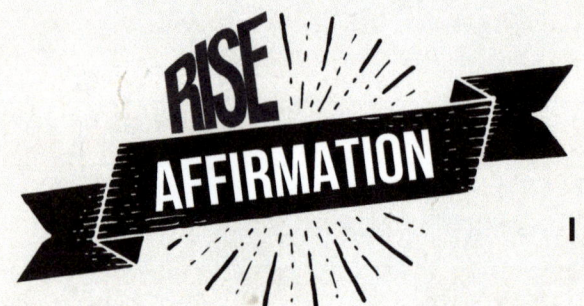

I am pure of heart.

Luke 7:34 (NLT) — "The Son of Man (Jesus), on the other hand, feasts, and drinks, and you say, 'He's a glutton and a drunkard, and a friend of tax collectors and other sinners!'"

Psalms 51:10 (NLT) — "Create in me a clean heart, O God. Renew a loyal spirit within me."

1 John 4:9-12 (NKJV) — "In this the love of God was manifested toward us, that God sent His only begotten Son into the world, that we might live through Him. In this is love, not that we loved God, but that He loved us and sent His Son to be the propitiation for our sins. Beloved, if God so loved us, we also ought to love one another. No one has seen God at any time. If we love one another, God abides in us, and His love has been perfected in us."

We're called to be a friend to sinners, to love like Jesus with pure hearts. Exploring and understanding our motivations is an important part of this journey to love others purely so take some time to read the prompts below that you can use for personal reflection with the Holy Spirit or discuss with a leader or small group.

1. How does examining our motives align with modeling the heart of Jesus and being a friend to those in need?

2. Why is it important to be aware of our intentions when connecting with others?

3. Share strategies and ideas for examining motives. What is a person's incentive or motivation to do a particular thing?

4. What are some external motivations?

5. What are some internal motivations?

DAY 10
DAY HIKE ON THE MOUNTAIN OF FAMILY

In this journey up the Mountain of Family, you truly know God as Papa. You have learned that God's love displayed looks like Strength. He wants you to know that you are accepted. You are not rejected. As God's heir, He is inviting you to partner with Him in bringing healing and restoration to families. God is asking you to identify obstacles or lies that hinder people from truly knowing Him as Papa God. He wants to display His love and healing through you. You have access to an authentic relationship with God, Creator of the Universe, and He is inviting you to partner with Him to bring the Kingdom to Earth. With the Holy Spirit as your guide, use the following prompts as you explore and discover God's assignment for you on the Mountain of Family.

Step 1: Based on what you've learned in your study of the Mountain of Family, express in your own words God's intent for this mountain.

Step 2: Take some time to investigate and observe various family activities, gatherings, and social interactions, or reflect on past experiences. What did you observe? Were your observations and experiences in alignment or out of alignment with The Truth about God on the Mountain of Family? How so?

Step 3: When reformers see problems or challenges, their response is to bring truth and Kingdom solutions for restoration. Ask the Holy Spirit to highlight areas on this mountain that need truth. What problem or challenge have you identified?

Step 4: Knowing that you are called by God to bring Kingdom solutions, ask the Holy Spirit for insight about the problem(s) or challenge(s) you've identified. Think about the essential understandings, affirmations, and insights that you've learned from your study on the Mountain of Family. What's one solution you can bring?

Step 5: How and with whom will you share your findings? How can you apply these lessons in your own life?

Work with your teacher or facilitator to determine how you will demonstrate your knowledge and understanding, for example, through the use of powerpoint presentation, written word, role play. With whom will you share your knowledge and understanding? It could be your family or your classmates. You might share on an online platform. You may even want to reach out to your pastor to share with the church or contact a decision-maker in your community or state.

MOUNTAIN OF RELIGION

CHAPTER 3

CHECK YOUR SUPPLIES

    Day 1 – The Face of God on the Mountain of Religion

    Day 2 – The Lie About God on the Mountain of Religion

    Day 3 – The Truth About God on the Mountain of Religion

BASECAMP ACTIVATIONS

    Day 4 – It's Not About Scoring Points

    Day 5 – Withdraw Judgment, Dare to Love

    Day 6 – False Religion Leaves Us Empty

    Day 7 – Don't Be Like the Pharisees

    Day 8 – Don't Pass Go without the Holy Spirit

    Day 9 – Everything Out of a Heart of Love

MOUNTAIN CLIMB

    Day 10 – Day Hike on the Mountain of Religion

DAY 1
THE FACE OF GOD ON THE MOUNTAIN OF RELIGION

I am a child of God who loves and honors others.

Revelation 5:12 (NKJV) — "Worthy is the Lamb that was slain to receive power and riches and wisdom and strength and HONOR and glory and blessing."

Romans 12:10 (NLT) — "Love each other with genuine affection and take delight in honoring each other."

John 13:34 (NKJV) — "A new commandment I give to you, that you love one another, as I have loved you; that you also love one another."

As we begin the climb on the Mountain of Religion, we'll discover God as our Redeemer. As you begin the climb, explore the questions below that you can use for personal reflection with the Holy Spirit or discuss with a leader or small group.

1. One of the greatest expressions of love we can share is pointing others to a loving Father and Creator. This is the very thing that a religious spirit likes to stand in the way of. Describe some ways you can express this kind of love in your everyday life?

2. Create a list of responses that you might share with others who reject your invitation to know God. Make sure they are responses that are accepting and loving and don't leave the other person feeling rejected.

DAY 2
THE LIE ABOUT GOD ON THE MOUNTAIN OF RELIGION

I am under the new covenant.

Matthew 11:30 (NLT) — "For My yoke is easy to bear, and the burden I give you is light."

2 Corinthians 3:6 (NLT) — "He has enabled us to be ministers of His new covenant. This is a covenant not of written laws, but of the Spirit. The old written covenant ends in death; but under the new covenant, the Spirit gives life."

Jeremiah 31:33-34 (NKJV) — 'But this is the covenant that I will make with the house of Israel after those days, says the Lord: I will put my law in their minds, and write it on their hearts; and I will be their God, and they shall be My people. No more shall every man teach his neighbor, and every man his brother, saying, 'Know the Lord,' for they all shall know Me, from the least of them to the greatest of them, says the Lord. For I will forgive their iniquity, and their sin I will remember no more."

On the Mountain of Religion, Satan uses a religious spirit to spread lies and false ideas about our relationship with God. Satan wants you on the hamster wheel of religion, constantly striving to try and know God and be good enough when instead we should focus on creating true intimacy with our Creator by surrendering our heart. Spend some time and use the prompts below for personal reflection with the Holy Spirit or discuss with a leader or small group.

1. The impossibility of keeping the letter of the law points us to our need of the One who fulfilled the law and gave us His Spirit as a guarantee. Describe the relief you might feel if you had been carrying a heavy weight and it had been lifted.

2. Explain what a religious spirit means to you. How do we show others that a relationship with God isn't about rules, laws, and "religion"?

3. What does it look like to live in freedom in the new covenant?

DAY 3
THE TRUTH ABOUT GOD ON THE MOUNTAIN OF RELIGION

I am eternally secure through Jesus Christ.

Revelation 12:7 (NLT) — "Then there was war in Heaven. Michael and his angels fought against the dragon and his angels."

Ephesians 2:8-9 (NLT) — "God saved you by His grace when you believed. And you can't take credit for this; it is a gift from God. Salvation is not a reward for the good things we have done, so none of us can boast about it."

John 10:28-29 (NKJV) — "And I give them eternal life, and they shall never perish; neither shall anyone snatch them out of my hand. My Father, who has given them to Me, is greater than all; and no one is able to snatch them out of My Father's hand."

Today, we learned about God as a redeemer and the sacrifice He made in order for us to be able to draw near to Him. Below are prompts that you can use for personal reflection with the Holy Spirit or discuss with a leader or small group.

1. Discover the meaning of your name if you don't already know. Your name, like the Archangel Michael, is significant. What did you learn about your name?

2. What might be its significance? Ask friends or your parents for their thoughts on your name.

3. Remind yourself of the Golden Rule found in Luke 6:31. Then paraphrase using the word honor.

4. How does that impact the meaning or make you think differently about it?

DAY 4
IT'S NOT ABOUT SCORING POINTS

You can give yourself permission to love unconditionally without an agenda.

I am able to love others without an agenda.

Mark 12:30 (NLT) — "And you must love the Lord your God with all your heart, all your soul, all your mind, and all your strength."

1 Corinthians 13:13 (NLT) — "Three things will last forever—faith, hope, and love—and the greatest of these is love."

1 Corinthians 16:14 (NKJV) — "Let all that you do be done in love."

As Christians, love is the agenda. It's not a race to see how many people we can get to Heaven. If we love others well, salvation will often come as a result. Spend some time reflecting on this idea and the prompts below with the Holy Spirit or with a leader or study group.

1. Why is it important to approach every conversation and interaction with love in mind rather than focused on what the outcome is going to be?

2. Have you ever experienced someone being nice to you, but you knew their motives weren't pure? How did that make you feel?

3. How does the love described in 1 Corinthians 13 differ from approaching others with an agenda or without the love of Jesus?

DAY 5
WITHDRAW JUDGMENT, DARE TO LOVE

You can live grateful and aware of your need for a Redeemer so that you aren't tempted to judge others.

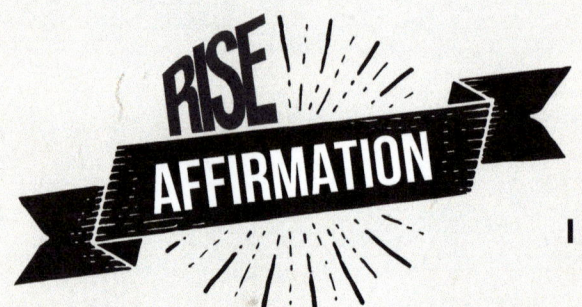

I am a judgement-free zone.

Isaiah 53:6 (NLT) — "All of us, like sheep, have strayed away. We have left God's paths to follow our own. Yet the Lord laid on Him the sins of us all."

I John 4:16 (NLT) — "We know how much God loves us, and we have put our trust in His love. God is love, and all who live in love live in God, and God lives in them."

Psalms 119:176 (NKJV) — "I have gone astray like a lost sheep; Seek Your servant, For I do not forget Your commandments."

Our judgment can affect others and sometimes even push them further from God, spend some time reflecting on the questions below with the Holy Spirit or discuss with a leader or small group.

1. Examine the words found in our prophetic Scripture—"Yet the Lord laid on Him the sins of us all." God stood in the gap for you and me and chose to sacrifice His only Son on the cross on our behalf. Take some time to imagine the gravity and intensity of that moment. What do you feel?

2. Discuss some of the different ways you can call people to a higher kingdom standard without judgment. Do you have the tendency to default to judge or love?

3. Think of a specific example where your default might have been to judge first and then think about how reacting with love could have helped the situation. Explain your answer.

DAY 6
FALSE RELIGION LEAVES US EMPTY

You can help others find the real God who is always near.

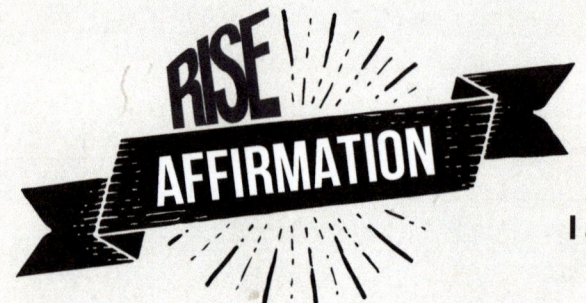

I am serving the one true God.

Psalms 145:18 (NIV) — "The Lord is near to all who call on Him."

John 3:16 (NLT) — "For this is how God loved the world: He gave his one and only Son, so that everyone who believes in him will not perish but have eternal life."

Isaiah 61:1-3 (NKJV) — "The Spirit of the Lord God is upon Me, because the Lord has anointed Me to preach good tidings to the poor; He has sent Me to heal the brokenhearted, to proclaim liberty to the captives, and the opening of the prison to those who are bound; to proclaim the acceptable year of the Lord, and the day of vengeance of our God; to comfort all who mourn, to console those who mourn in Zion, to give them beauty for ashes, the oil of joy for mourning, the garment of praise for the spirit of heaviness; that they may be called trees of righteousness, the planting of the Lord, that He may be glorified."

Today, we talked about how false gods or idols will only leave us feeling empty and even more disconnected from God. As you think about what God requires of you and the consequences of putting your faith in false gods, read the questions below and spend some time reflecting on the questions below with the Holy Spirit or discuss them with a leader or small group.

1. How does the practice of false religions, including playing church, where you have to work hard or perform to earn your place, create a sense of distance between a person and the Creator God of the Bible who loves us unconditionally?

2. How can understanding the deception and disconnection caused by false religion lead us to feel compassion instead of judgment towards another person?

DAY 7
DON'T BE LIKE THE PHARISEES

You cannot help others get free from a religious spirit if you don't first recognize it in yourself.

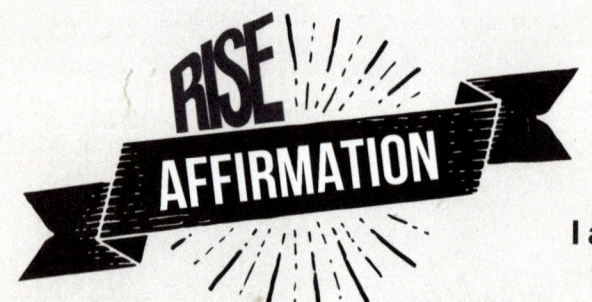

I am free from spiritual pride.

Luke 12:1 (NLT) — "Beware of the yeast of the Pharisees—their hypocrisy."

James 4:6 (NLT) — "God opposes the proud but gives grace to the humble."

1 John 4:1 (NKJV) — "Beloved, do not believe every spirit, but test the spirits, whether they are of God; because many false prophets have gone out into the world."

Being able to recognize a religious spirit and embodying humility instead of pride can help us avoid being led astray and leading others down the path with us. Use the questions below for personal reflection with the Holy Spirit or discuss with a leader or small group.

1. In what ways have you seen the religious spirit active in someone else or in yourself? How did it make you feel?

2. Think of a time when you let your pride take over instead of humbling yourself. How could you have handled the situation differently?

3. How can we avoid becoming a hypocrite like the Pharisees? What practical steps can we take to cultivate humility and avoid the trappings of a religious spirit?

4. How can we reflect the true nature of God through our actions and attitudes?

DAY 8
DON'T PASS GO WITHOUT THE HOLY SPIRIT

UNDERSTANDING

The transformation of the world comes through the power of the Holy Spirit in you.

I am filled with the Holy Spirit.

John 16:7 (NKJV) — "It is to your advantage that I go away; for if I do not go away, the Helper will not come to you; but if I depart, I will send Him to you."

Acts 1:8 (NLT) — "But you will receive power when the Holy Spirit comes upon you."

Romans 8:9 (NKJV) — "But you are not in the flesh but in the Spirit, if indeed the Spirit of God dwells in you. Now if anyone does not have the Spirit of Christ, he is not His."

Today, we talked about the Holy Spirit, how to invite the Holy Spirit into your life, and how the Holy Spirit will guide and teach us. As you reflect on our need to be filled with the Holy Spirit, reflect on the prompts below on your own with the Holy Spirit or with a leader or small group.

1. Why is it important to seek an encounter with the Holy Spirit?

2. How can we cultivate a deeper connection with the Holy Spirit through worship, prayer, and personal reflection?

3. Why is it important to ask for an infilling of the Holy Spirit?

4. Consider manifestations of the Holy Spirit you have experienced, witnessed, or read about. How does a person's life change when they receive power from the Holy Spirit?

5. How does the Holy Spirit transform us?

DAY 9
EVERYTHING OUT OF A HEART OF LOVE

You have been empowered by the Holy Spirit to promote a relationship, not a religion.

I am wildly and passionately in love with Jesus.

Revelation 2:4-5 (TPT) — "I have this against you: you have abandoned the passionate love you had for me at the beginning. Think about how far you have fallen! Repent and do the works *of love* you did at first."

Matthew 24:12 (NKJV) — "Because lawlessness will abound, the love of many will grow cold."

As you reflect on the difference between promoting religion and promoting a relationship with God, explore the prompts below and use them for personal reflection with the Holy Spirit or discuss with a leader or small group.

1. How does an 'all in' kind of love for Jesus enable us to experience the supernatural power of God in our daily lives?

2. How can our love for God guide and impact our actions, decisions, and interactions with others?

DAY 10
DAY HIKE ON THE MOUNTAIN OF RELIGION

In this journey up the Mountain of Religion, you truly know God as Redeemer. You have learned that God's love looks like Honor. The free gift of redemption and eternal life have been given to you. God's gift of the Cross making way for redemption for all is available. God has called us to be ministers of this new covenant by loving Him, ourselves, and others, without judgment. God is asking you to identify obstacles or lies that hinder people from having an authentic relationship with Him based on love and grace and not laws and rules. You have access to an authentic relationship with God, Creator of the Universe, and He is inviting you to partner with Him to bring Kingdom to Earth. With the Holy Spirit as your guide, use the following prompts as you explore and discover God's assignment for you on the Mountain of Religion.

Step 1: Based on what you've learned in your study of the Mountain of Religion, express in your own words God's intent for this mountain.

Step 2: Take some time to investigate and observe various church activities you may have been involved in, or even gatherings and social interactions where spirituality was the topic of discussion. What did you observe? Were your observations and experiences in alignment or out of alignment with The Truth about God on the Mountain of Religion? How so?

Step 3: When reformers see problems or challenges, their response is to bring truth and

Kingdom solutions for restoration. Ask the Holy Spirit to highlight areas on this mountain that need truth. What problem or challenge have you identified?

Step 4: Knowing that you're called by God to bring Kingdom solutions, ask the Holy Spirit for insight about the problem(s) or challenge(s) you've identified. Think about the essential understandings, affirmations, and insights that you've learned from your study on the Mountain of Religion. What is one solution you can bring?

Step 5: How (method of demonstration) and with whom (audience) will you share your findings?

Work with your teacher or facilitator to determine how you'll demonstrate your knowledge and understanding, for example, through the use of powerpoint presentation, written word, role play. With whom will you share your knowledge and understanding? It could be your family or your classmates. You might share on an online platform. You may even want to reach out to your pastor to share with the church or contact a decision-maker in your community or state.

MOUNTAIN OF EDUCATION

CHAPTER 4

CHECK YOUR SUPPLIES

Day 1 – The Face of God on the Mountain of Education

Day 2 – The Lie About God on the Mountain of Education

Day 3 – The Truth About God on the Mountain of Education

BASECAMP ACTIVATIONS

Day 4 – Relationship Before Everything

Day 5 – It's All About Your Story

Day 6 – The Never-Ending Path of Discovery

Day 7 – Who's Driving This Thing Anyway?

Day 8 – Questions Are Us

Day 9 – What's So Special About You?

MOUNTAIN CLIMB

Day 10 – Day Hike on the Mountain of Education

DAY 1
THE FACE OF GOD ON THE MOUNTAIN OF EDUCATION

I am teachable.

Psalms 139: 17-18 (NLT) — "How precious are Your thoughts about me, O God. They cannot be numbered! I can't even count them; they outnumber the grains of sand! And when I wake up, You are still with me!"

Revelation 5:12 (NLT) — "Worthy is the Lamb who was slaughtered to receive power and riches and WISDOM and strength and honor and glory and blessing."

Exodus 4:11-12 (NKJV) — "So the Lord said to him, 'Who has made man's mouth? Or who makes the mute, the deaf, the seeing, or the blind? Have not I, the Lord? Now therefore, go, and I will be with your mouth and teach you what you shall say."

On this mountain, we'll discover God as Teacher. God wants to teach you important things because you are important to Him and He wants you to unlock your potential and story for His glory. Take some time reflecting on the questions below and how the lessons on this mountain can apply to your life, whether you intend to climb this mountain of culture or a different one.

1. Discuss the reality of Psalms 139:17-18. What does that even look like to you?

2. How does the truth of the vastness of Creator God who chooses to be close and intimate with you make you feel?

3. You are a co-creator in your own learning. If you were able to share with your teacher the different ways in which you learn best, what would you tell them?

DAY 2
THE LIE ABOUT GOD ON THE MOUNTAIN OF EDUCATION

I am wise when I am completely dependent on God.

Proverbs 12:15 (NLT) — "Fools think their own way is right, but the wise listen to others."

2 Timothy 1:7 (NLT) — "For God has not given us a spirit of fear and timidity, but of power, love, and self-discipline."

Psalms 32:8 (NKJV) — "I will instruct you and teach you in the way you should go; I will guide you with My eye."

RISE MOUNTAIN CLIMBER MEETUP

A big part of the journey on the Mountain of Education is learning to let go of fear and the need to be self-reliant. Relying too much on ourselves and feeding into the lie that we are on our own instead of trusting God is how corruption on the Mountain of Education thrives. Spend some time reflecting on the questions below with the Holy Spirit or with a leader or small group.

1. Explain your process for accessing information and knowledge.

2. Does your ability to find knowledge with just the touch of a few keys on a keyboard distract you from seeking answers from God?

3. Compare and contrast subjects you study in school. How do you protect yourself by discerning or filtering the material that has been given to you?

4. Do you accept anything that you hear at face value? If so, why could this be a concern?

DAY 3
THE TRUTH ABOUT GOD ON THE MOUNTAIN OF EDUCATION

I am important to God.

Deuteronomy 29:29 (NKJV) — "The secret things belong to the LORD our God, but those things which are revealed belong to us and to our children forever, that we may do all the words of this law."

Daniel 2:30 (NLT) — "And it is not because I am wiser than anyone else that I know the secret of your dream, but because God wants you to understand what was in your heart."

James 3:13 (NKJV) — "Who is wise and understanding among you? Let him show by good conduct that his works are done in the meekness of wisdom."

True wisdom is dependence on God and the knowledge that we're important to Him. Through basic curiosity, spending time with God, and asking questions, you can begin to unlock the secrets meant just for you and your story. Use the prompts we've provided to do some personal reflection with the Holy Spirit or with a leader or small group. Always feel free to go further than the questions, journaling your thoughts and ideas as you explore the mountains and listen for God's voice to direct you.

1. Describe what it means to depend on God for wisdom.

2. What strategies do you practice or have in place to ensure you are receiving wisdom from God?

3. Discuss uncovering the mysteries and secrets hidden for you. What does that look like?

4. What might be God's purpose in hiding secrets away for you to find?

DAY 4
RELATIONSHIP BEFORE EVERYTHING

UNDERSTANDING

I learn best when the teacher-student relationship is prioritized.

AFFIRMATION

I am relational like God.

ANCHOR

1 John 2:27 (NLT) — "But you have received the Holy Spirit, and He lives within you, so you don't need anyone to teach you what is true. For the Spirit teaches you everything you need to know, and what He teaches is true--it is not a lie. So just as He has taught you, remain in fellowship with Christ."

Psalms 46:1 (NLT) — "God is our refuge and strength, always ready to help in times of trouble."

Isaiah 54:13 (NKJV) — "All your children shall be taught by the Lord, and great shall be the peace of your children."

It's a fact that we learn better when we actively engage with what we're learning and if we have a relationship of trust with the teacher imparting knowledge. It's important to filter the information you receive and examine it rather than just accepting it as truth. Ask God for wisdom and discernment as you learn and work through the questions below.

1. How can you integrate faith and relationship with God into your learning journey?

2. How does your relationship with God help you evaluate and filter the information that you take in everyday?

3. Reflecting on your own learning experiences, what roles has relationship played in your ability to truly understand and apply what you have learned?

4. How can you further cultivate meaningful relationship to enhance your journey?

DAY 5
IT'S ALL ABOUT YOUR STORY

An education that makes room for your unique qualities will help you tell your unique story.

I am filling the earth with the knowledge of God.

Habakkuk 2:14 (NKJV) — "For the earth will be filled with the knowledge of the glory of the Lord, as the waters cover the sea."

Mark 11:24 (NLT) — "I tell you, you can pray for anything, and if you believe that you've received it, it will be yours."

Micah 4:2 (NKJV) — "Many nations shall come and say, 'Come, and let us go up to the mountain of the Lord, to the house of the God of Jacob; He will teach us His ways, and we shall walk in His paths.' For out of Zion the law shall go forth, and the word of the Lord from Jerusalem."

Discouragement, distraction, doubt, and division are all tools used by the enemy to keep you from discovering your unique potential and story and to keep you from sharing it for God's glory. Being mindful of this as you climb your mountain will leave you better equipped to stay firm in the truth of God's goodness and the pursuit of your unique story. Spend some time using the questions below for personal reflection with the Holy Spirit or discuss with a leader or small group.

1. Reflecting on the idea that God wants to show Himself through you and your story, what does it mean to have a purpose in the world?

2. How can your unique story contribute to the knowledge of the glory of God filling the earth?

DAY 6
THE NEVER-ENDING PATH OF DISCOVERY

You can play your important role in God's story when you are taught to use both sides of your brain.

I am in a constant state of discovery.

John 6:12 (NLT) — "After everyone was full, Jesus told his disciples, "Now gather the leftovers, so that nothing is wasted."

Exodus 35:31 (NLT) — "The Lord has filled Bezalel with the Spirit of God, giving him great wisdom, ability, and expertise in all kinds of crafts."

Today we talked about the two sides of your brain and their different functions and attributes. It's important to use both sides of your brain as you learn and stay in a constant state of discovery. Answer some questions to discover how you learn best and begin to strategize how you can become stronger in all areas of your thinking.

1. How does having a growth mindset contribute to the process of continual discovery and pursuing the limitless God?

2. In what ways can you cultivate a growth mindset in your own life?

3. We learned that God equips individuals with specific skills and abilities in order to complete their life's work. What specific skills and abilities do you recognize in your own life?

4. How do you think these will empower you to do what God has called you to do?

DAY 7
WHO'S DRIVING THIS THING ANYWAY?

As a student, you should have input and be involved in your learning experience.

I am a co-designer of my learning.

Proverbs 22:6 (NLT) — "Direct your children onto the right path, and when they are older, they will not leave it."

Jeremiah 33:3 (NLT) — "Ask Me and I will tell you remarkable secrets you do not know about things to come."

Taking ownership of your own learning means actively participating and taking the initiative to ask questions and let your curiosity drive you to explore your ideas. True curiosity and learning create an ability to problem solve and think critically, as well as unpack, rearrange, and reimagine ideas or problems with an open mind or out-of-the-box thinking. Spend some time to reflect on your learning experience up to this point with the questions provided.

1. Do you feel you have taken ownership of your learning? Why or why not?

2. Discuss the different strategies and opportunities that you can begin to explore in order to take ownership of your learning.

3. Why is it important to ask questions, share ideas, and provide input in the learning process?

4. How does your active involvement contribute to a more meaningful and personalized learning experience?

DAY 8
QUESTIONS ARE US

You can ask questions in order to gain wisdom.

I am full of questions that will make me wise.

Proverbs 4:7 (NKJV)— "Wisdom is the principal thing; therefore, get wisdom. And in all your getting, get understanding."

Matthew 7:7 (NLT) — "Keep on asking, and you will receive what you ask for. Keep on seeking, and you will find. Keep on knocking, and the door will be opened to you."

Proverbs 20:5 (NKJV) — "Counsel in the heart of a man is like deep water, but a man of understanding will draw it out."

Wisdom is the ability to do something with what we know and to have true wisdom you have to ask questions. Spend some time on the questions below for personal reflection with the Holy Spirit on the prompts provided or discuss them with a leader or small group.

1. How has the emphasis on test scores and memorization in education affected your learning experience?

2. In what ways do you think this approach has hindered the development of your wisdom and understanding?

3. How can the practice of asking questions contribute to the growth of wisdom and understanding?

4. In what ways can you take responsibility for your learning?

DAY 9
WHAT'S SO SPECIAL ABOUT YOU?

Discovering your passions and gifts helps you discover your purpose and path.

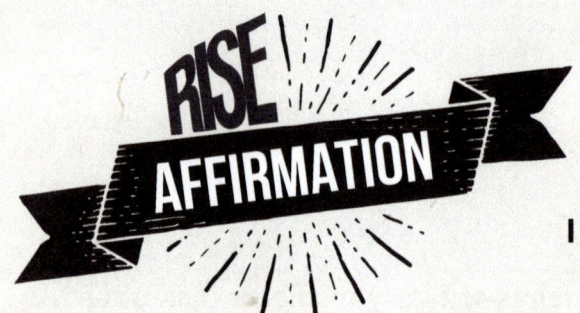

I am special.

1 Peter 4:10-11 (NLT) — "God has given each of you a gift from his great variety of spiritual gifts. Use them well to serve one another. Do you have the gift of speaking? Then speak as though God Himself were speaking through you. Do you have the gift of helping others? Do it with all the strength and energy that God supplies. Then everything you do will bring glory to God through Jesus Christ. All glory and power to Him forever and ever! Amen."

Psalms 139:14 (NLT) — "Thank you for making me so wonderfully complex! Your workmanship is marvelous—how well I know it."

Isaiah 48:17-18 (NKJV) — "Thus says the Lord, your Redeemer, The Holy One of Israel; 'I am the Lord your God, Who teaches you to profit, Who leads you by the way you should go. Oh, that you had heeded My commandments! Then your peace would have been like a river, and your righteousness like the waves of the sea."

It's time to discover how you learn best and what makes you special! Use the questions below to conduct a survey and discover more about yourself!

1. Conduct a survey of five of your closest friends or family members. Ask three questions: What are the gifts and talents that you recognize inside of me? When you think of me, what is one thing that immediately comes to mind? What is something you think that I do better than most people you know? Share your findings.

2. How can you identify and recognize your spiritual gifting?

3. What practices or experiences can help you discern the unique ways in which God has equipped you to serve others?

DAY 10
DAY HIKE ON THE MOUNTAIN OF EDUCATION

In this journey up the Mountain of Education, you truly know God as Teacher. You have learned that God's love displayed looks like Wisdom. He wants you to know how important you are to Him. He has written a story about you, and He wants the whole world to know it. His plan is that when they know you, they will know Him. You only need to remain. Your charge is to tell your story for His glory, drawing others to Him. You have access to an authentic relationship with God, Creator of the Universe, and He is inviting you to partner with Him to bring Kingdom to Earth. With the Holy Spirit as your guide, use the following prompts as you explore and discover God's assignment for you on the Mountain of Education.

Step 1: Based on what you have learned in your study of the Mountain of Education, express in your own words God's intent for this mountain.

Step 2: Take some time to investigate and observe various learning experiences you have had, perhaps a school you have attended. What did you observe? Were your observations and experiences in alignment or out of alignment with The Truth about God on the Mountain of Education? How so?

Step 3: When reformers see problems or challenges, their response is to bring truth and

Kingdom solutions for restoration. Ask the Holy Spirit to highlight areas on this mountain that need truth. What problem or challenge have you identified?

Step 4: Knowing that you are called by God to bring Kingdom solutions, ask the Holy Spirit for insight about the problem(s) or challenge(s) you have identified. Think about the essential understandings, affirmations, and insights that you've learned from your study on the Mountain of Education. What is one solution you can bring?

Step 5: How (method of demonstration) and with whom (audience) will you share your findings?

Work with your teacher or facilitator to determine how you will demonstrate your knowledge and understanding, for example, through the use of powerpoint presentation, written word, or role play. With whom will you share your knowledge and understanding? It could be your family or your classmates. You might share on an online platform. You may even want to reach out to your pastor to share with the church or contact a decision-maker in your community or state.

MOUNTAIN OF ECONOMY

CHAPTER 5

CHECK YOUR SUPPLIES

- Day 1 – The Face of God on the Mountain of Economy
- Day 2 – The Lie About God on the Mountain of Economy
- Day 3 – The Truth About God on the Mountain of Economy

BASECAMP ACTIVATIONS

- Day 4 – God Makes the Best Business Partner
- Day 5 – The Trust Standard
- Day 6 – Loved Displayed as Riches
- Day 7 – This Is Not a Competition
- Day 8 – More Than We Might Ask or Think
- Day 9 – The Better Way

MOUNTAIN CLIMB

- Day 10 – Day Hike on the Mountain of Economy

DAY 1
THE FACE OF GOD ON THE MOUNTAIN OF ECONOMY

I am a channel for riches to flow through to others.

Luke 6:38 (NLT) — "Give, and you will receive. Your gift will return to you in full—pressed down, shaken together to make room for more, running over, and poured into your lap. The amount you give will determine the amount you get back."

Revelation 5:12 (NLT) — "Worthy is the Lamb that was slaughtered to receive power and RICHES and wisdom and strength and honor and glory and blessing."

Deuteronomy 15:10 (NKJV) — "You shall surely give to him, and your heart should not be grieved when you give to him, because for this thing the Lord your God will bless you in all your works and in all to which you put your hand."

As we begin our climb up the Mountain of Economy, we're going to learn about God as Provider. A key component of God as Provider is generosity, as we are called to be generous to others and display God's provision through our story. Take some time reflecting on the questions below and how the lessons on this mountain can apply to your life, whether you intend to climb this mountain of culture or a different one.

1. Explain why it might be difficult to trust God for provision. Have you ever taken matters into your own hands, made a bad decision with your money, and then felt bad about asking God to help you out?

2. Categorize the different areas of your life where you or your family need financial provision. Are there items in these categories that you take for granted and assume will always be there?

3. Are you seeking God's wisdom about His provision in these areas?

DAY 2
THE LIE ABOUT GOD ON THE MOUNTAIN OF ECONOMY

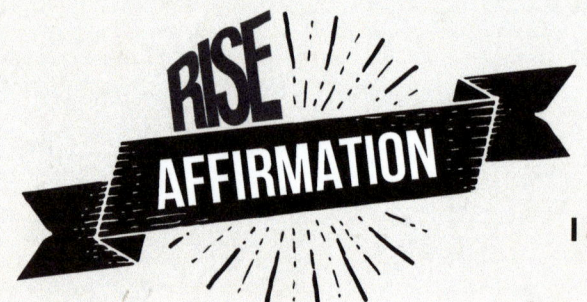

I am trusting in God as my provider.

Matthew 6:24 (NLT) — "No one can serve two masters. For you will hate one and love the other, you will be devoted to one and despise the other. You cannot serve God and be enslaved to money."

Haggai 2:8 (NLT) — "The silver is mine, and the gold is mine, says the LORD of Heaven's Armies."

Isaiah 12:2 (NKJV) — "Behold, God is my salvation, I will trust and not be afraid; 'for Yah, the Lord, is my strength and song; He also has become my salvation.'"

On the Mountain of Economy, Satan tries to convince us that if we're in need, we have to provide for ourselves. He wants to inspire greed and convince us to hoard our wealth and count on our own ability to gain and keep it, but this is counter to the truth that God will provide for us. Spend some time reflecting on the questions provided with the Holy Spirit or with a leader or small group.

1. Talk about a time in your life when it felt like all hope was lost and you felt like God wasn't there. What did it feel like? How did you respond?

2. How do you combat the lie of feeling alone and unprovided for? What is the truth?

3. How does God want us to respond to times of "need?"

DAY 3
THE TRUTH ABOUT GOD ON THE MOUNTAIN OF ECONOMY

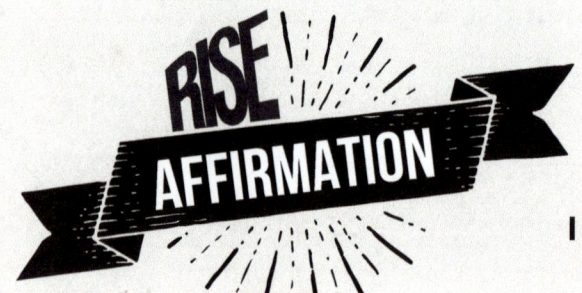

I am provided for.

Genesis 22:14 (NLT) — "Abraham named the place Yahweh-Yireh (which means "the Lord will provide")."

Philippians 4:19 (NLT) — "And this same God who takes care of me will supply all your needs from His glorious riches which have been given to us in Christ Jesus."

Deuteronomy 8:18 (NKJV) — "And you shall remember the Lord your God, for it is He who gives you power to get wealth, that He may establish His covenant which He swore to your fathers, as it is this day."

Understanding God as Provider impacts everything about the way we treat our finances and the decisions we make. Trusting in God's provision instead of relying on ourselves can make all the difference. Use the questions below for personal reflection with the Holy Spirit or discuss with a leader or small group.

1. Compare and contrast a mindset of abundance to one of lack and scarcity. What are some ways you can move towards a mindset of abundance?

2. Think of a specific need in your community. It is your charge to gather friends to help meet the need. What is your plan?

DAY 4
GOD MAKES THE BEST BUSINESS PARTNER

You must work hard in business but work harder to believe in His supernatural abilities to help you as you do your part.

I am a generous giver.

Proverbs 3:9 (NLT) — "Honor the Lord with your wealth and with the best part of everything you produce."

2 Corinthians 9:7-8 (NLT) — "You must each decide in your heart how much to give. And don't give reluctantly or in response to pressure. For God loves a person who gives cheerfully. And God will generously provide all you need. Then you will always have everything you need, and plenty left over to share with others."

God doesn't just provide for ministry; He financially supports all things that are Kingdom and there's a million different ways outside of ministry to bring God's Kingdom and better ways to Earth. Explore the questions below and think about how your various interests can help bring God's ways to that area.

1. How does Jesus' demonstration of generosity and abundance reflect the nature of our Father in Heaven?

2. How might we model the same generosity in our own lives?

3. How can integrity and excellence in handling finances contribute to our partnership with God?

4. What are some ways we can trust Him in these areas?

5. Our society, through social media, is flooded with the next new thing, the latest technology. How does this challenge your ability to discern, value, and practice integrity in finances?

DAY 5
THE TRUST STANDARD

You must value your trust in God more than your ability to get or keep wealth. This is doing business God's way.

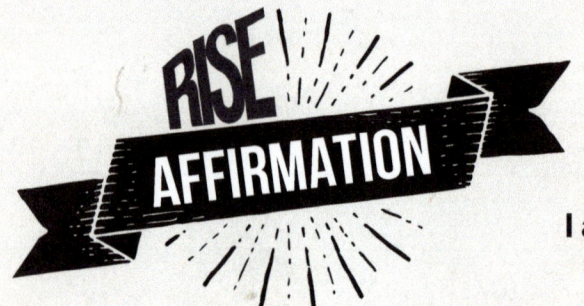

I am cultivating trust in God.

Deuteronomy 8:18 (NKJV) — "Remember the LORD your God, for it is He who gives you power to get wealth."

Proverbs 3:5-6 (NLT) — "Trust in the LORD with all your heart; do not depend on your own understanding. Seek His will in all you do, and He will show you which path to take."

1 Chronicles 29:12 (NKJV) — "Both riches and honor come from You, and You reign over all. In Your hand is power and might; In Your hand it is to make great and to give strength to all."

Trust is the currency that God's provision flows through; it will always be required when conducting Kingdom business. Explore the questions below and begin to uncover how cultivating trust in Him is the key to climbing the Mountain of Economy.

1. Envision what it would be like if you trusted God for wealth and at some point in your life, He gave you the power to become wealthy. What kinds of tests do you think you would need to go through in life to arrive at that point?

2. Recount a time when you or your family were unsure of what path to take, and you sought God about it instead of trying to figure it out yourself. In what ways did He show you the best path?

DAY 6
LOVE DISPLAYED AS RICHES

You can use your wealth to solve problems in any area of life, not just inside the four walls of the church.

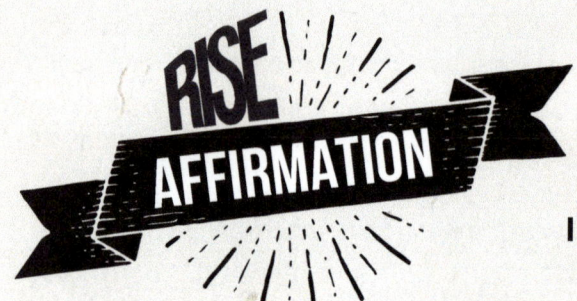

I am love displayed as riches.

Matthew 25:40 (NLT) — "I tell you the truth, when you did it to one of the least of these my brothers and sisters, you were doing it to me!"

1 Corinthians 10:31 (NLT) — "Whatever you do, do it all for the glory of God."

Deuteronomy 15:7-8 (NKJV) — "If there is among you a poor man of your brethren, within any of the gates in your land which the Lord your God is giving you, you shall not harden your heart nor shut your hand from your poor brother, but you shall open your hand wide to him and willingly lend him sufficient for his need, whatever he need."

Now that you've consider how provision doesn't just mean providing for things related to religion and can extend far beyond that, spend some time exploring different areas or problems that you could help solve!

1. As representatives of God, how can we display love through riches in every area of life and on any of the mountains of culture?

2. What are some examples of how finances can be used to solve societal problems and alleviate pain?

3. Have you felt a calling to help or provide somewhere?

4. Spend some time praying and journaling about where God might be calling you to help others on this mountain.

DAY 7
THIS IS NOT A COMPETITION

You can be successful in business without being greedy or competitive.

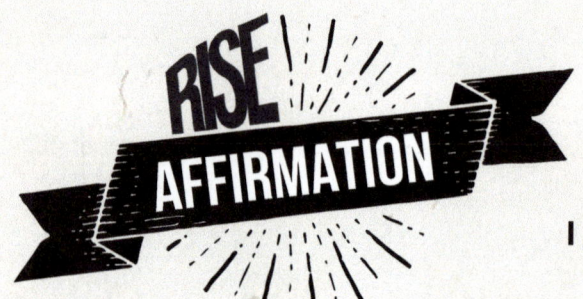

I am not driven by meaningless competition.

Ecclesiastes 4:4 (NLT) — "I observed that most people are motivated to success because they envy their neighbors. But this, too, is meaningless—like chasing the wind."

1 Corinthians 9:25 (NLT) — "All athletes are disciplined in their training. They do it to win a prize that will fade away, but we do it for an eternal prize."

1 Timothy 6:8-9 (NKJV) — "And having food and clothing, with these we shall be content. But those who desire to be rich fall into temptation and a snare, and into many foolish and harmful lusts which drown men in destruction and perdition."

Gaining wealth is not a competition, someone else having it does not prevent us from having it too; it's not the goal. Spend some time reflecting on how competition can impact and promote greed through the questions below.

1. Describe the feelings of competition you have experienced. Was your motivation to be excellent and to do all for the glory of God, or was it for recognition and to show that you were better than the other person?

2. List ways we can strive for greatness without falling into greed.

3. What are some acceptable motivations for doing well?

4. Does doing your best always have to be equated with winning?

DAY 8
MORE THAN WE MIGHT ASK OR THINK

Your work was meant to be your life's calling.

I am partners with a limitless God.

1 Timothy 1:17 (NKJV) — "Now to the King eternal, immortal, invisible, to God who alone is wise, be honor and glory forever and ever. Amen."

Ephesians 3:20 (NLT) — "Now all glory to God, who is able, through his mighty power at work within us, to accomplish infinitely more than we might ask or think."

Our work is meant to be more than just work, it's meant to be our calling. It's meant to fulfill us and help us spread God's good news and better ways across the mountains of culture. As you reflect on your lesson and what you've learned so far on the Mountain of Economy, reflect on the discussion questions below.

1. Discuss your journey in trusting God, your Provider—the eternal, immortal, invisible God—with your story. How does knowing that God loves you fully and completely influence your outlook on your life's calling?

2. Can you think of examples from history or contemporary society where individuals have embraced their unique calling and made a significant impact? What lessons can you learn from their stories?

DAY 9
THE BETTER WAY

You have an advantage in business as a follower of Jesus when you handle finances God's better way.

I am choosing God's better way.

Ezekiel 28:4 (NLT) — "With your wisdom and understanding you have amassed great wealth—gold and silver for your treasuries."

Proverbs 3:13-15 (NIV) — "Blessed are those who find wisdom, those who gain understanding, for she is more profitable than silver and yields better returns than gold. She is more precious than rubies; nothing you desire can compare with her."

Proverbs 4:7-10 (NKJV) — "Wisdom is the principal thing; Therefore, get wisdom. And in all your getting, get understanding. Exalt her, and she will promote you; She will bring you honor, when you embrace her. She will place on your head an ornament of grace; A crown of glory she will deliver to you. Hear, my son, and receive my sayings, and the years of your life will be many."

Obeying God even when it seems silly or doesn't make sense is all a part of putting your faith and trust in Him. If you ignore His nudges, you could miss out on great opportunities by missing where He was trying to lead you. Spend some time on the discussion questions below as you prepare to begin climbing the Mountain of Economy.

1. What steps can you take to seek God's wisdom before making financial decisions, whether in your personal life or in business?

2. How can you develop a practice of choosing the better way in financial matters?

3. Reflect on a financial decision you've made in the past. How do you think seeking God's wisdom could have influenced the outcome? How can you apply this lesson in the future?

DAY 10
DAY HIKE ON THE MOUNTAIN OF ECONOMY

In this journey up the Mountain of Economy, you truly know God as Provider. You have learned that God's love is displayed as Riches. He wants us to be confident in His provision for us and loves when we allow Him to provide for others through us. Trusting God with our everything and learning to trade in His Kingdom economy will bring the return that no one will be able to deny. You have access to an authentic relationship with God, Creator of the Universe, and He is inviting you to partner with Him to bring Kingdom to Earth. With the Holy Spirit as your guide, use the following prompts as you explore and discover God's assignment for you on the Mountain of Economy.

Step 1: Based on what you've learned in your study of Mountain of Economy, express in your own words God's intent for this mountain.

Step 2: Take some time to observe and reflect on how you see people making and using money, even their attitudes about it. Don't forget to consider yourself, your own family, and the community around you. What did you observe? Were your observations and experiences in or out of alignment with The Truth about God on the Mountain of Economy? How so?

Step 3: When reformers see problems or challenges, their response is to bring truth and Kingdom solutions for restoration. Ask the Holy Spirit to highlight areas on this mountain that need truth. What problem or challenge have you identified?

Step 4: Knowing that you're called by God to bring Kingdom solutions, ask the Holy Spirit for insight about the problem(s) or challenge(s) you've identified. Think about the essential understandings, affirmations, and insights that you've learned from your study on the Mountain of Economy. What is one solution you can bring?

Step 5: How (method of demonstration) and with whom (audience) will you share your findings?

Work with your teacher or facilitator to determine how you will demonstrate your knowledge and understanding, for example, through the use of powerpoint presentation, written word, role play. With whom will you share your knowledge and understanding? It could be your family or your classmates. You might share on an online platform. You may even want to reach out to your pastor to share with the church or contact a decision-maker in your community or state.

MOUNTAIN OF ARTS & ENTERTAINMENT

CHAPTER 6

CHECK YOUR SUPPLIES

Day 1 – The Face of God on the Mountain of Arts & Entertainment

Day 2 – The Lie About God on the Mountain of Arts & Entertainment

Day 3 – The Truth About God on the Mountain of Arts & Entertainment

BASECAMP ACTIVATIONS

Day 4 – A Vow to Protect, Not Compromise

Day 5 – Guard Your Heart

Day 6 – Don't Get Blinded by the Spotlight

Day 7 – Shine the Light

Day 8 – Creativity, It's in Your DNA

Day 9 – Pursue Authenticity and Excellence of Character

MOUNTAIN CLIMB

Day 10 – Day Hike on the Mountain of Arts & Entertainment

DAY 1
THE FACE OF GOD ON THE MOUNTAIN OF ARTS & ENTERTAINMENT

I am a display of God's glory.

John 1:3 (NLT) — "God created everything through Him, and nothing was created except through Him."

Revelation 5:12 (NLT) — "Worthy is the Lamb that was slaughtered to receive power and riches and wisdom and strength and honor and GLORY and blessing."

Psalms 19:1 (NKJV) — "The heavens declare the glory of God; And the firmament of heaven shows His handiwork."

As we begin our climb up the Mountain of Arts & Entertainment, we're going to learn about God as Creator and how He's gifted us with this same creative ability! Take some time reflecting on the questions below and how the lessons on this mountain can apply to your life, whether you intend to climb this mountain of culture or a different one.

1. Knowing that Creator God lives within us, how can we approach creativity without being religious, but acknowledging the work God is doing through us?

2. The creative power God has placed inside of you has the ability to counter darkness. Think of an area in arts & entertainment where darkness is evident, what would be a creative response to counter?

DAY 2
THE LIE ABOUT GOD ON THE MOUNTAIN OF ARTS & ENTERTAINMENT

I am fun-loving.

John 10:10b (NKJV) — "I have come that they may have life, and that they may have it more abundantly."

Psalms 16:11 (NKJV) — "In Your presence is fullness of joy, and at Your right hand are pleasures forevermore."

Ecclesiastes 8:15 (ESV) — "And I commend joy, for man has nothing better under the sun but to eat and drink and be joyful, for this will go with him in his toil through the days of his life that God has given him under the sun."

On the Mountain of Arts & Entertainment, Satan tries to spread lies about God and that He doesn't want us to have fun. Satan wants to convince us that joy isn't found in God or in Godly things. Spend some time using the prompts below for personal reflection with the Holy Spirit or discuss with a leader or small group and think about the types of art and entertainment you currently enjoy.

1. Discuss what it looks like to bring the abundant life of God into arts & entertainment. How can you partner with Heaven to do your part in bringing God's better ways to arts, entertainment, or sports?

2. The Kingdom of God is righteousness, peace, and joy. No fun = no joy. Describe the enemy's strategy in wanting you to believe that God doesn't want you to have fun. What would be his motive?

DAY 3
THE TRUTH ABOUT GOD ON THE MOUNTAIN OF ARTS & ENTERTAINMENT

I am enjoyed by God.

Romans 14:17 (NKJV) — "For the Kingdom of God is...righteousness, peace, and joy in the Holy Spirit."

Luke 12:32 (NKJV) — "...It is your Father's good pleasure to give you the kingdom."

Psalms 149:3-4 (ESV) — "Let them praise his name with dancing, making melody to Him with tambourine and lyre! For the Lord takes pleasure in his people; he adorns the humble with salvation.

The truth is God wants us to have fun! He wants us to be creative and experience all the joy life and He has to offer us. Take some time to read the discussion questions below and spend time reflecting with the Holy Spirit or a mentor or small group.

1. Consider the truth that God wants you to have fun. Do you believe this? What is the evidence of it in your life?

2. Create a plan for bringing creativity and joy into your family or community. How can we approach the Mountain of Arts & Entertainment with a kingdom perspective?

3. How has culture corrupted art and entertainment?

DAY 4
A VOW TO PROTECT, NOT COMPROMISE

You can have a positive impact in Arts & Entertainment by protecting your standards of purity and morality.

I am creative like God.

Philippians 4:8 (NLT) — "Fix your thoughts on what is true, and honorable, and right, and pure, and lovely, and admirable. Think about things that are excellent and worthy of praise."

Philippians 2:3-4 (NLT) — "Don't be selfish; don't try to impress others. Be humble, thinking of others as better than yourselves. Don't look out only for your own interests, but take an interest in others, too."

Understanding how to have fun and be creative without compromising your integrity or values can be a struggle when we're surrounded by entertainment that does compromise our values. Explore the questions below and take time to reflect with the Holy Spirit.

1. Consider examples of how someone might use their creative gifting in a compromised way. What are some different ways in the Mountain of Arts & Entertainment you see this taking place? What is your response when you see this happening?

2. What are creative solutions to countering compromise in arts and entertainment?

3. How can you use your creativity in the area of arts and entertainment to present a life-giving message?

4. How can you use it to support storytelling and display God's glory?

DAY 5
GUARD YOUR HEART

You must guard your heart and produce the fruit of the Holy Spirit in order to promote God's glory.

I am producing the fruit of the Holy Spirit.

Proverbs 4:23 (NIV) — "Guard your heart above all else, for it determines the course of your life."

Galatians 5:22 (NLT) — "But the Holy Spirit produces this kind of fruit in our lives: love, joy, peace, patience, kindness, goodness, faithfulness, gentleness, and self-control."

Romans 15:13 (ESV) — "May the God of hope fill you with all joy and peace in believing, so that by the power of the Holy Spirit you may abound in hope."

Write out the fruits of the spirit from your book as well as the check-in questions. Spend some time reflecting on those questions and the discussion questions below with the Holy Spirit or a trusted leader or small group.

1. How has the enemy used our creativity and love for entertainment to erode the moral fabric of society?

2. In what ways, can those called to arts and entertainment help restore it?

3. How can the fruit of the Spirit serve as a Biblical standard for evaluating the impact of your work in arts and entertainment?

4. How can you ensure that your work and creative expressions align with the fruit of the Spirit and bring life to the world?

DAY 6
DON'T GET BLINDED BY THE SPOTLIGHT

You can be in the spotlight when you give the glory back to God.

I am showing off God.

Daniel 1:20 (NLT) — "Whenever the king consulted them [referring to Daniel and his friends] in any matter requiring wisdom and balanced judgment, he found them ten times more capable than any of the magicians and enchanters in his entire kingdom."

Daniel 2:27-28a (NLT) — "There are no wise men, enchanters, magicians, or fortune-tellers who can reveal the king's secret, but there is a God in heaven who reveals mysteries. He has shown King Nebuchadnezzar what will happen in days to come."

Galatians 6:14 (NKJV) — "But God forbid that I should boast except in the cross of the Lord Jesus Christ, by whom the world has been crucified to me, and I to the world."

Maybe you're interested in being in the spotlight on the Mountain of Arts & Entertainment or maybe you'd prefer something creative outside of the spotlight but either way, knowing how the public eye or even the eyes of just a few people can influence you is important to know. Spend some time reflecting on the discussion questions below.

1. How can you develop the ability to listen to God's guidance and obey His timing, even when it means pausing your own aspirations for recognition?

2. Evaluate the arts and entertainment you spend your time with. Are these reflective of Kingdom values? Why or why not?

DAY 7
SHINE THE LIGHT

You can use your light to promote the Light of God and true freedom to the world.

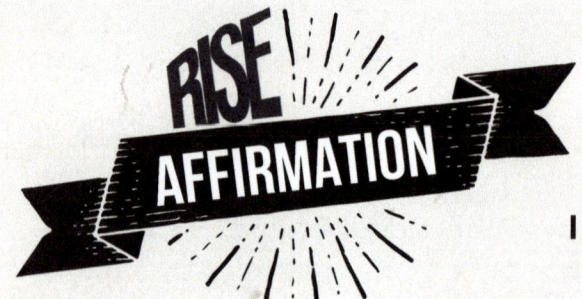

I am a bright light shining.

John 1:5 (NLT) — "The light shines in the darkness, and the darkness can never extinguish it."

John 8:36 (NLT) — "So, if the Son sets you free, you are truly free."

Acts 13:47 (NKJV) — "For so the Lord has commanded us: 'I have set you as a light to the Gentiles, that you should be for salvation to the ends of the earth.'"

We can all be a light for God and His Kingdom, both within this mountain of culture and within others, and only by pressing into our freedom in Christ can we shine our light! Take some time reviewing the discussion questions below and reflect with the Holy Spirit, trusted mentor, or small group.

1. Are you ready for the spotlight? In what ways can being in the spotlight prematurely be a setup from the enemy?

2. How can we be the focus of attention and recognition and not let selfishness and pride enter in?

3. What are some important disciplines and practices we can put in place to ensure we are not blinded by the spotlight?

4. What does it mean to be a "glory carrier" on the Mountain of Arts & Entertainment?

DAY 8
CREATIVITY, IT'S IN YOUR DNA

You can go to God for a limitless supply of creativity.

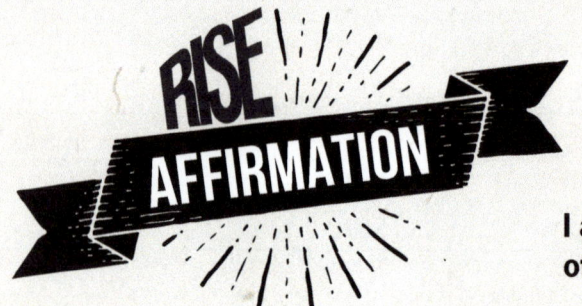

I am connected to a limitless supply of creativity.

Isaiah 64:4 (NLT) — "No ear has heard and no eye has seen a God like you, who works for those who wait for him!"

Isaiah 55:9 (NLT) — "For just as the heavens are higher than the earth, so My ways are higher than your ways and My thoughts higher than your thoughts."

Psalms 31:19 (NKJV) — "Oh, how great is Your goodness, which You have laid up for those who fear You, which You have prepared for those who trust in You in the presence of the sons of men!"

As we face challenges on the mountains of culture, looking to God and spending time with the Holy Spirit is important for finding our purpose and staying on the right path. Take some time to think about what it means to trust God to access what you need and reflect on the questions below.

1. Discuss the challenge to believe amongst the greatest odds. What happens when we partner with God and believe He will do mighty things through us?

2. Do you struggle to see what is not yet seen?

3. How can you ask Him to help you?

4. How does tapping into the limitless supply of God's creativity impact your own creative abilities?

DAY 9
PURSUE AUTHENTICITY AND EXCELLENCE OF CHARACTER

You can make a difference by being your authentic self and pursuing excellence of character.

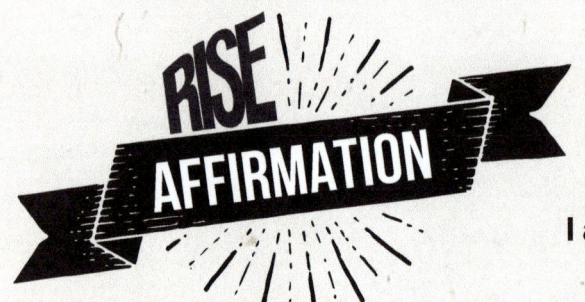

I am authentic.

1 Corinthians 6:19 (NKJV) — "Your body is a temple of the Holy Spirit who is in you, whom you have from God and you are not your own."

1 Samuel 16:7 (NLT) — "People judge by outward appearance, but the Lord looks at the heart."

Most likely, you've experienced a time where you struggled to be your authentic self in the face of others. Explore the questions below and take time for personal reflection with the Holy Spirit.

1. Consider a time when you tried to act like someone that you knew you weren't. How did it make you feel? What was your motivation for doing this?

2. How does finding your authentic self and committing to excellent character enhance your creativity, ideas, and unique expression?

DAY 10
DAY HIKE ON THE MOUNTAIN OF ARTS & ENTERTAINMENT

In this journey up the Mountain of Arts & Entertainment, you truly know God as Creator. You have learned that God's love displayed looks like Glory. He wants you to have fun and enjoy your life. He has given you a canvas to paint the world for His glory, making Him shine bright to those around us. It's in our DNA. Heaven is an endless reservoir of creative resources as we engage with our spirit and imagination. You have access to an authentic relationship with God, Creator of the Universe, and He is inviting you to partner with Him to bring Kingdom to Earth. With the Holy Spirit as your guide, use the following prompts as you explore and discover God's assignment for you on the Mountain of Arts & Entertainment.

Step 1: Based on what you have learned in your study of the Mountain of Arts & Entertainment section, express in your own words God's intent for this mountain.

Step 2: Take some time to consider the creativity that surrounds you every day— design, art, dance, nature, films, or movies. What did you observe? Were your observations and experiences in alignment or out of alignment with The Truth about God on the Mountain of Arts & Entertainment? How so?

Step 3: When reformers see problems or challenges, their response is to bring truth and Kingdom solutions for restoration. Ask the Holy Spirit to highlight areas on this mountain that need truth. What problem or challenge have you identified?

Step 4: Knowing that you are called by God to bring Kingdom solutions, ask the Holy Spirit for insight about the problem(s) or challenge(s) you have identified. Think about the essential understandings, affirmations, and insights that you've learned from your study on the Mountain of Arts & Entertainment. What is one solution you can bring?

Step 5: How (method of demonstration) and with whom (audience) will you share your findings?

Work with your teacher or facilitator to determine how you will demonstrate your knowledge and understanding, for example, through the use of powerpoint presentation, written word, role play. With whom will you share your knowledge and understanding? It could be your family or your classmates. You might share on an online platform. You may even want to reach out to your pastor to share with the church or contact a decision-maker in your community or state.

MOUNTAIN OF MEDIA

CHAPTER 7

CHECK YOUR SUPPLIES

Day 1 – The Face of God on the Mountain of Media

Day 2 – The Lie About God on the Mountain of Media

Day 3 – The Truth About God on the Mountain of Media

BASECAMP ACTIVATIONS

Day 4 – What Goes In, Will Come Out

Day 5 – Shout It from the Mountaintops

Day 6 – Peace Rules Over Fear

Day 7 – Be a Part of the Solution, Not the Problem

Day 8 – A Climber Is a Digger

Day 9 – The Ultimate Caretaker

MOUNTAIN CLIMB

Day 10 – Day Hike on the Mountain of Media

DAY 1
THE FACE OF GOD ON THE MOUNTAIN OF MEDIA

I am a blessing to others.

Revelation 5:12 (NLT) — "Worthy is the Lamb who was slaughtered— to receive power and riches and wisdom and strength and honor and glory and BLESSING."

Jeremiah 29:11 (NLT) — "For I know the plans I have for you," says the Lord. "They are plans for good and not for disaster, to give you a future and a hope."

Hebrews 13:16 (NKJV) — "But do not forget to do good and to share, for with such sacrifices God is well pleased."

On the Mountain of Media, we're meant to know God as Communicator. Hearing God or finding the path He's trying to lead you to can be difficult. Calling on the Holy Spirit to know the truth of God and spending time in His presence is the best way to hear Him. Take some time to reflect on the prompts below regarding the Mountain of Media.

1. Discuss ways the news media has impacted your beliefs about God.

2. In what ways are we not believing these truths about Him because of how news and social media is presented through the media?

3. Sound carries frequency. Reflect on the media (music, noise, voices) that you allow into your mind and spirit, then consider the frequency of your own life. Are you experiencing shame, guilt, anger, fear, and anger or are you experiencing courage, gratitude, joy, abundance, and peace? Share your reflections.

DAY 2
THE LIE ABOUT GOD ON THE MOUNTAIN OF MEDIA

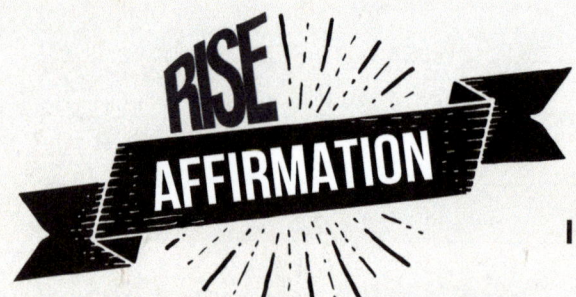

I am not afraid.

John 10:10 (NLT) — "The thief does not come except to steal, and to kill, and to destroy. I have come that they may have life, and that they may have it more abundantly."

2 Timothy 1:7 (NLT) — "For God has not given us a spirit of fear, but of power and of love and of a sound mind."

Psalms 56:3-4 (NKJV) — "Whenever I am afraid, I will trust in You. In God (I will praise His word), In God I have put my trust; I will not fear. What can flesh do to me?"

Have you ever felt like God didn't have a good plan for you? Like you were alone or abandoned? These are the lies that Satan tries to spread to sow doubt in us about God's love and care for us. Explore the questions below and take some time to reflect with the Holy Spirit, a leader, or small group.

1. Share where fear has played a role in your life. How can the truth that God gives us power, love, and a sound mind help you conquer this fear?

2. Describe perfect love and how it protects against fear.

DAY 3
THE TRUTH ABOUT GOD ON THE MOUNTAIN OF MEDIA

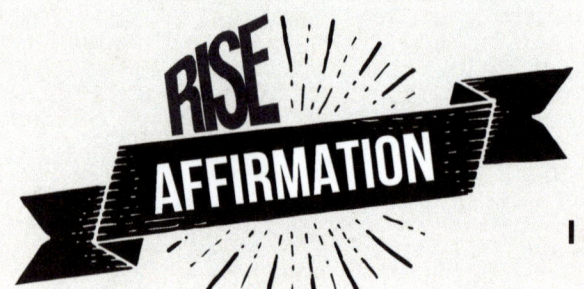

I am hopeful.

Philippians 1:6 (NLT) — "And I am certain that God, who began the good work within you, will continue His work until it is finally finished on the day when Christ Jesus returns."

Jeremiah 29:11 (NLT) — "'For I know the plans I have for you,' says the LORD. 'They are plans for good and not for disaster, to give you a future and a hope.'"

RISE MOUNTAIN CLIMBER MEETUP

God does have a good plan for you; He wants good things for you because He loves you. As you hold onto this truth, take a look at the questions below.

1. Define intentionality.

2. How might you be intentional about partnering with God to see His good plan in your life manifested?

3. What does it look like?

4. What are the different steps and strategies you need to put in place to realize God's plan for your life?

5. What are the different resources (prophetic words, assets, relationships, scriptures, declarations) that you have or are believing in that will help move you forward and keep the vision?

DAY 4
WHAT GOES IN, WILL COME OUT

You can use your words to intentionally communicate life.

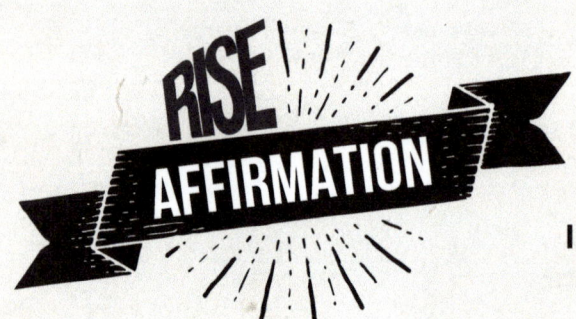

I am careful with how I use my words.

Proverbs 18:21 (NLT) — "The tongue can bring death or life; those who love to talk will reap the consequences."

Luke 6:45 (NLT) — "A good person produces good things from the treasury of a good heart, and an evil person produces evil things from the treasury of an evil heart. What you say flows from what is in your heart."

Proverbs 10:19 (NKJV) — "In the multitude of words sin is not lacking, but he who restrains his lips is wise."

Being mindful about what we're consuming in all areas of life and consciously speaking life instead of death is important in all areas but especially on the Mountain of Media. Reflect on the questions below with the Holy Spirit or a leader or small group.

1. Why is it so important for influencers on the Mountain of Media to be mindful of what they focus on, consume, and spend their time on?

2. How can these choices influence your heart?

3. Discuss the treasury of your heart. What are the precious things found there?

4. Are there any things stored there that need to be removed?

DAY 5
SHOUT IT FROM THE MOUNTAINTOPS

UNDERSTANDING

You can neutralize bad news with good news and a hopeful perspective.

AFFIRMATION

I am bringing the good news to the Seven Mountains.

ANCHOR

Proverbs 15:30 (NLT) — "A cheerful look brings joy to the heart; good news makes for good health."

Isaiah 52:7 (NLT) — "How beautiful on the mountains are the feet of the messenger who brings good news."

Psalms 71:17 (NKJV) — "O God, You have taught me from my youth; and to this day I declare Your wonderous works."

As you think about the Mountain of Media and the news stories you hear every day, does your experience reflect this idea of spreading fear? Do you get caught up in the constant negativity of the news cycle and find yourself wondering where God is in all of this? Grounding yourself in the truth of God's love for us and the knowledge that He does have a plan that will all work out for good is the best way to begin combatting that fear as we try to climb the Mountain of Media. The discussion questions below will help you to explore more on the Mountain of Media.

1. What is a narrative or lie that media has told you about your generation?

2. How does having a hopeful perspective about your own life enable you to bring hope to others?

3. Why is it important to believe in God's best about yourself as you share with others?

4. Do you believe God's best about you?

DAY 6
PEACE RULES OVER FEAR

UNDERSTANDING — You can make a difference in media by bringing peace and encouragement.

AFFIRMATION — I am an encourager.

ANCHOR — **Ephesians 4:29** (NLT) — "Don't use foul or abusive language. Let everything you say be good and helpful, so that your words will be an encouragement to those who hear them."

John 14:27 (NKJV) — "Peace I leave with you, My peace I give to you; not as the world gives do I give to you. Let not your heart be troubled, neither let it be afraid."

1 Peter 3:8-9 (NKJV) — "Finally, all of you be of one mind, having compassion for one another; love as brothers, be tenderhearted, be courteous, not returning evil for evil or reviling for reviling, but on the contrary blessing, knowing that you were called to this, that you may inherit a blessing."

Focusing on the good and the hopeful parts of a story, even in the midst of tragedy or hardship is how we can combat the lies on the Mountain of Media that Satan tries to spread. Every story can be redeemed by God and used for good. Take some time to review the questions below and reflect on them with the Holy Spirit or a trusted mentor.

1. How does echoing a hopeful narrative from the mountaintop have the power of change things and bring peace instead of fear?

2. How can we show up on the Mountain of Media and replace fear with peace?

3. How can our actions and excellence speak louder than words in demonstrating God's love?

DAY 7
BE A PART OF THE SOLUTION, NOT THE PROBLEM

 **UNDERSTANDING**

You can bring Kingdom solutions to the problems in society.

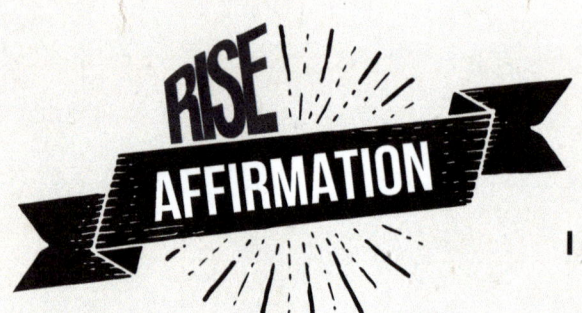 **AFFIRMATION**

I am a problem solver.

 **ANCHOR**

Matthew 6:10 (ESV) — "Your Kingdom come, Your will be done, on Earth as it is in Heaven."

Revelation 5:12 (NLT) — "Worthy is the Lamb that was slaughtered to receive power and riches and wisdom and strength and honor and glory and BLESSING."

James 1:5 (NKJV) — "If any of you lacks wisdom, let him ask of God, who gives to all liberally and without reproach, and it will be given to him."

By ensuring that we're contributing Kingdom solutions to our mountains of culture, we can bring real change and be part of the solution, not the problem! Spend time reflecting on the discussion questions below and think about everything we've learned about the Mountains of Culture so far.

1. Choose one of the mountains we have studied. It can be the Mountain of Media or another. Identify a problem in that area of culture that needs a Kingdom solution. Describe your solution and why you believe it is Kingdom.

2. What are your unique gifts and talents you have identified? How can you utilize them to contribute to the Kingdom solution?

DAY 8
A CLIMBER IS A DIGGER

You can help others discover the goodness of God when you find and report the story behind the obvious story.

I am a truth digger.

I Corinthians 2:7 (NLT) — "No, the wisdom we speak of is the mystery of God—His plan that was previously hidden, even though He made it for our ultimate glory before the world began."

Colossians 1:26 (NLT) — "This message was kept secret for centuries and generations past, but now it has been revealed to God's people."

2 Timothy 2:15-16 (NKJV) — "Be diligent to present yourself approved to God, a worker who does not need to be ashamed, rightly dividing the word of truth. But shun profane and idle babblings, for they will increase to more ungodliness."

Sometimes finding the good within a sad or tragic story can be difficult. We have to look past the obvious and dig deeper to try and discover where we can find hope within these stories. Explore the questions below and use some time for personal reflection with the Holy Spirit or a trusted mentor.

1. How does the concept of being a "story-ologist" connect to the exploration of hidden truths and the mysteries of God?

2. What are some of the mysteries you have discovered? Have you been on any treasure hunts lately with God?

3. What are the risks of only looking at things on the surface?

4. What are the benefits of digging deep and uncovering unknown parts of a story?

DAY 9
THE ULTIMATE CARETAKER

 UNDERSTANDING

You are not called to carry the weight of the world.

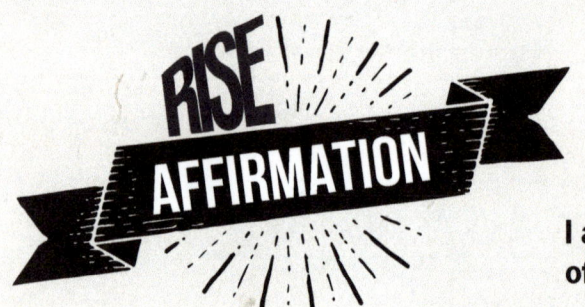 AFFIRMATION

I am a responsible reporter of news.

 ANCHOR

2 Corinthians 12:9 (NKJV) — "My grace is sufficient for you, for My strength is made perfect in weakness."

1 Peter 5:7 (NLT) — "Give all your worries and cares to God, for He cares about you".

James 1:18 (NKJV) — "Of His own will He brought us forth by the word of truth, that we might be a kind of first fruits of His creatures."

It's almost time to start your climb on the Mountain of Media. Reflect on all the lessons we've covered so far and how it all works together to help us make the climb. Use the questions below to prepare yourself to start climbing!

1. Describe the different ways you have heard the Lord speak to you about your specific calling. What have you heard?

2. How has this understanding impacted your voice on the Mountain of Media?

3. What is the difference between being overwhelmed by something and being sensitive to it?

4. How does being grounded in the truth of God help us maintain sensitivity without becoming overwhelmed?

DAY 10
DAY HIKE ON THE MOUNTAIN OF MEDIA

In this journey up the Mountain of Media, you truly know God as Communicator. You have learned how God's love displayed looks like Blessing. He wants to use your voice to be that blessing to others as we turn their hearts towards His good plan for them. Shining brightly – our God reflection—before and to others. You have access to an authentic relationship with God, Creator of the Universe, and He is inviting you to partner with Him to bring Kingdom to Earth. With the Holy Spirit as your guide, use the following prompts as you explore and discover God's assignment for you on the Mountain of Media.

Step 1: Based on what you have learned in your study of the Mountain of Media, express in your own words God's intent for this mountain.

Step 2: Take some time to consider and reflect on the voices that are coming at you through media each and every day—it could be by the company you keep or the social media platforms you engage. What did you observe? Were your observations and experiences in alignment or out of alignment with The Truth about God on the Mountain of Media? How so?

Step 3: When reformers see problems or challenges, their response is to bring truth and Kingdom solutions for restoration. Ask the Holy Spirit to highlight areas on this mountain that need truth. What problem or challenge have you identified?

Step 4: Knowing that you are called by God to bring Kingdom solutions, ask the Holy Spirit for insight about the problem(s) or challenge(s) you have identified. Think about the essential understandings, affirmations, and insights that you've learned from your study on the Mountain of Media. What is one solution you can bring?

Step 5: How (method of demonstration) and with whom (audience) will you share your findings?

Work with your teacher or facilitator to determine how you will demonstrate your knowledge and understanding, for example, through the use of powerpoint presentation, written word, role play. With whom will you share your knowledge and understanding? It could be your family or your classmates. You might share on an online platform. You may even want to reach out to your pastor to share with the church or contact a decision-maker in your community or state.

MOUNTAIN OF GOVERNMENT

CHAPTER 8

CHECK YOUR SUPPLIES

    Day 1 – The Face of God on the Mountain of Government

    Day 2 – The Lie About God on the Mountain of Government

    Day 3 – The Truth About God on the Mountain of Government

BASECAMP ACTIVATIONS

    Day 4 – The King Loves Justice

    Day 5 – Values Over Ideals

    Day 6 – Kings Produce Kingly Solutions

    Day 7 – Lead With Love

    Day 8 – Life Speak

    Day 9 – Ruling Is Serving

MOUNTAIN CLIMB

    Day 10 – Day Hike on the Mountain of Government

DAY 1
THE FACE OF GOD ON THE MOUNTAIN OF GOVERNMENT

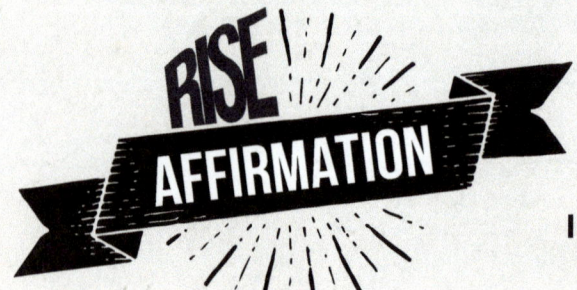

I am a child of the King.

Matthew 20:28 (NLT) — "The Son of Man did not come to be served, but to serve, and to give His life a ransom for many."

Revelation 5:12 (NLT) — "Worthy is the Lamb that was slaughtered to receive POWER and riches and wisdom and strength and honor and glory and blessing."

Galatians 3:26 (NKJV) — "For you are all sons of God through faith in Christ Jesus."

On the Mountain of Government, we're meant to know God as King. Understanding God as our King is important to understand our own role in the kingdom but also his great love for us as his children and royal heirs! Take some time to reflect on the prompts below with the Holy Spirit or with a trusted mentor.

1. Share an example of how a government, past or present, used their power positively or negatively.

2. Did you have any examples that aligned with the incorrupt power of God? Did they use control and manipulation?

DAY 2
THE LIE ABOUT GOD ON THE MOUNTAIN OF GOVERNMENT

I am against government corruption.

Proverbs 29:2 (NLT) — "When the Godly are in authority, the people rejoice. But when the wicked are in power, they groan."

Isaiah 9:6 (NLT) — "For a child is born to us, a son is given to us. The government will rest on his shoulders. And he will be called: Wonderful Counselor, Mighty God, Everlasting Father, Prince of Peace."

Romans 12:2 (NKJV) — "And do not be conformed to this world, but be transformed by the renewing of your mind, that you may prove what is that good and acceptable and perfect will of God."

In this lesson we learned about the lies that Satan tries to spread through the Mountain of Government, pushing us further from God and His better ways. As you check your supplies on the Mountain of Government and think about your own experiences with this mountain so far, spend some time in personal reflection with the Holy Spirit, small group, or leader.

1. Discuss the reality of what the government is like in your nation.

2. Based on your government and the leaders, do the citizens feel like they are truly cared about?

3. List things that are potentially corrupt in your government and things that are Kingdom about your government.

DAY 3
THE TRUTH ABOUT GOD ON THE MOUNTAIN OF GOVERNMENT

I am royalty.

Matthew 6:30 (NLT) — "And if God cares so wonderfully for wildflowers that are here today and thrown into the fire tomorrow, He will certainly care for you. Why do you have so little faith?"

2 Corinthians 3:17 (NLT) — "For the Lord is the Spirit, and where the Spirit of the Lord is, there is freedom."

Romans 8:37-40 (NKJV) — "Yet in all these things, we are more than conquerors through Him who loved us. For I am persuaded that neither death nor life, nor angels nor principalities nor powers, nor things present nor things to come, nor height nor depth, nor any other created thing, shall be able to separate us from the love of God which is in Christ Jesus our Lord."

While the Mountain of Government can be an intimidating one, we need Kingdom reformers in all areas of culture to help produce change and bring God's better ways to Earth. The Truth on the Mountain of Government is that we are royalty and we have the power of our Heavenly Father and King on our side. As you think about the truth of God on the Mountain of Government, look at your discussion questions below and take time to reflect with the Holy Spirit or a trusted leader.

1. Differentiate between internal freedom versus external freedom.

2. How does the internal override the external?

3. What does this mean for your daily life?

4. How can being internally free (absent of the fear of judgment and rejection) impact your different relationships and how you communicate with others?

DAY 4
THE KING LOVES JUSTICE

You can learn to love justice and righteousness like our King does.

I am a lover of justice and righteousness.

Psalms 99:4 (NIV) — "The King is mighty, He loves justice."

Romans 14:17 (NLT) — "For the Kingdom of God is not a matter of eating and drinking, but of righteousness, peace and joy in the Holy Spirit."

Psalms 97:6 (NLT) — "The heavens proclaim His righteousness; every nation sees His glory."

Being on the Mountain of Government involves the same type of servant leadership required in all other mountains. Even as we find our purpose on one of the mountains of culture, we're still called to love like Jesus and care about others the way He cared for them. We must fight for justice and righteousness while being an example of God's love and character. Spend some time on the discussion questions below and reflect with the Holy Spirit or a trusted mentor or small group.

1. Describe your understanding of justice.

2. Why do you think it is something God loves?

3. What is the difference between God's justice and the world's justice?

4. What are ways you've seen justice abused in our world?

5. How can we interfere with God's justice?

DAY 5
VALUES OVER IDEALS

You must focus on your own character and morals when you are in a position of authority to keep you from the temptation to compromise.

I am guided by my values.

1 Corinthians 10:12 (NLT) — "If you think you are standing strong, be careful not to fall."

Proverbs 16:18 (NLT) — "Pride goes before destruction, and haughtiness before a fall."

Holding onto your morals and convictions in the face of attacks and criticism can be hard but it's essential for bringing change, especially to the Mountain of Government. On this mountain, you must be guided by your values and place your trust in Him and the Holy Spirit. Spend some time reflecting on the prompts below as you think about how to bring God's Kingdom to the Mountain of Government.

1. How does recognizing your values help you identify what needs changing and what part God wants to work on next?

2. In what ways can knowing our values help us partner with God to see change in our society?

3. How can pride contribute to corruption among leaders in government?

4. How does humility protect leaders from falling into destructive behaviors?

5. How can you apply these understandings to your own life?

DAY 6
KINGS PRODUCE KINGLY SOLUTIONS

You are going to need God's solutions for government because they are too big for us.

I am a representative of Heaven.

1 Peter 2:9 (NLT) — "But you are not like that, for you are a chosen people. You are royal priests, a holy nation, God's very own possession. As a result, you can show others the goodness of God, for He called you out of the darkness into His wonderful light."

Psalms 89:14 (NLT) — "Righteousness and justice are the foundation of Your throne. Unfailing love and truth walk before You as attendants."

1 Timothy 4:12 (NKJV) — "Let no one despise your youth, but be an example to the believers in word, in conduct, in love, in spirit, in faith, in purity."

As we climb all the mountains of culture, relying on God for wisdom and kingly solutions is how we're able to bring His Kingdom to Earth. Discuss the questions below with a leader or small group or spend some time in personal reflection with the Holy Spirit.

1. Think about the courtrooms in your own government. Are they characterized by righteousness, justice, and the love of truth?

2. In what ways can we bring Godly traits into the justice system in practical real-life ways?

3. How does the concept of being a chosen people, royal priests, and a holy nation impact your understanding of your role in society?

DAY 7
LEAD WITH LOVE

You must come under the power of God's love in order to lead with the power of love.

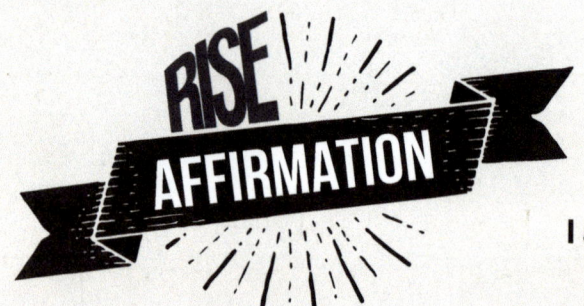

I am leading with love.

2 Timothy 1:7 (NLT) — "For God has not given us a spirit of fear and timidity, but of power, love, and self-discipline."

Exodus 15:12-13 (NLT) — "You raised Your right hand, and the Earth swallowed our enemies. With Your unfailing love You lead the people You have redeemed. In Your might You guide them to Your sacred home."

Psalms 136: 26 (NKJV) — "Oh, give thanks to the God of heaven! For His mercy endures forever."

It always comes back to love, and loving others even if they may not have the same beliefs that we do. We're to be a light for the world and an example of God's faithful love. As we strive to bring God's better ways to the Mountain of Government, we can bring these solutions with grace and love, always asking God for His wisdom to speak through us. Consider the discussion questions below with the Holy Spirit, a mentor, or a small group.

1. Consider those in authority in your local, state, or federal government. Do you see them leading with fear and manipulation or with love?

2. How does this impact you or your family?

3. What are some things that you can do to protect yourself against fear and manipulation?

4. Reflect on what we have learned about the love of God. Leading with love is not something we can do with our own efforts or strength. How do we lead with love with God's guidance?

5. What are ways we can lead with love absent of fear?

DAY 8
LIFE SPEAK

You will have more influence when you don't just say the right things, but actually do the right things.

I am a person whose actions speak louder than words.

1 John 3:18 (NLT) — "Dear children, let's not merely say that we love each other; let us show the truth by our actions."

James 2:26 (NLT) — "Just as the body is dead without breath, so also faith is dead without good works."

James 2:14-17 (NKJV) — "What does it profit, my brethren, if someone says he has faith but does not have works? Can faith save him? If a brother or sister is naked and destitute of daily food, and one of you says to them, 'Depart in peace, be warmed and filled,' but you do not give them the things which are needed for the body, what does it profit? Thus also faith by itself, if it does not have works, is dead."

More than anything we say, our actions show who we truly are and what we believe. As you reflect on this lesson and think on your life and what your actions reflect about you, reflect on the questions below with the Holy Spirit or with a trusted leader or small group.

1. How does the idea of displaying love through actions align with the concept of "actions speak louder than words"?

2. Describe the importance of faith in your daily walk with God. How is faith "dead" without good works? What is James talking about in terms of our faith?

DAY 9
RULING IS SERVING

You weren't created to dominate or rule over people, but over Satan and his principalities and demons.

I am salt and light.

Jeremiah 29:7 (NKJV) — "And seek the peace of the city where I have caused you to be carried away captive, and pray to the Lord for it; for in its peace you will have peace."

Matthew 5:13-16 (NLT) — "You are the salt of the earth. But what good is salt if it has lost its flavor? Can you make it salty again? It will be thrown out and trampled underfoot as worthless. You are the light of the world—like a city on a hilltop that cannot be hidden. No one lights a lamp and then puts it under a basket. Instead, a lamp is placed on a stand, where it gives light to everyone in the house. In the same way, let your good deeds shine out for all to see, so that everyone will praise your heavenly Father."

John 9:5 (NKJV) — "As long as I am in the world, I am the light of the world."

It's almost time to start the climb up your final mountain. As you spend time with the Holy Spirit and reflect on what it means to be the salt and light of the Earth, spend some time answering the questions below.

1. Design a job description for a City Planner (government servants who help plan communities so that they are good places to live) using what you have learned about loving and serving.

2. What "city" has God assigned you? What is your assignment there?

3. How does the metaphor of being salt and light in Matthew 5:13-16 illustrate our role in society?

4. What happens when we lose our flavor or hide our light?

5. How does our influence help preserve society and reveal Jesus and His Kingdom?

DAY 10
DAY HIKE ON THE MOUNTAIN OF GOVERNMENT

In this journey up the Mountain of Government, you truly know God as King. You have learned that God's love displayed looks like Power. He wants you to know that real power only comes from Him. Your charge is to step into your kingship, to lead with love, and to serve with humility so that you can see the transference of that power. You have access to an authentic relationship with God, Creator of the Universe, and He is inviting you to partner with Him to bring Kingdom to Earth. With the Holy Spirit as your guide, use the following prompts as you explore and discover God's assignment for you on the Mountain of Government.

Step 1: Based on what you have learned in your study of Mountain of Government, express in your own words God's intent for this mountain.

Step 2: Take some time to investigate and observe the way government operates in the different places that affect you and your family—the mayor's office, city council, school board, senators, and representatives. What did you observe? Were your observations and experiences in alignment or out of alignment with The Truth about God on the Mountain of Government? How so?

Step 3: When reformers see problems or challenges, their response is to bring truth and

Kingdom solutions for restoration. Ask the Holy Spirit to highlight areas on this mountain that need truth. What problem or challenge have you identified?

Step 4: Knowing that you are called by God to bring Kingdom solutions, ask the Holy Spirit for insight about the problem(s) or challenge(s) you have identified. Think about the essential understandings, affirmations, and insights that you've learned from your study on the Mountain of Government. What is one solution you can bring?

Step 5: How (method of demonstration) and with whom (audience) will you share your findings?

Work with your teacher or facilitator to determine how you will demonstrate your knowledge and understanding, for example, through the use of powerpoint presentation, written word, role play. With whom will you share your knowledge and understanding? It could be your family or your classmates. You might share on an online platform. You may even want to reach out to your pastor to share with the church or contact a decision-maker in your community or state.

YOU ARE A GENERATION OF REFORMERS

CHAPTER 9

Day 1 – Arise and Shine!

Day 2 – All the Children of the World

Day 3 – Oaks of Righteousness

Day 4 – Mercy Reigns Over Judgment

Day 5 – Prayer Is Not Enough

Day 6 – Grace, Grace, God's Grace

Day 7 – Friend of Sinners

Day 8 – Celebrate!

Day 9 – Prisoners of Hope

Day 10 – Get Up and Show Up!

DAY 1
ARISE AND SHINE!

 **UNDERSTANDING** — You understand the importance of taking what you know into the world to be a light shining forth.

 **AFFIRMATION** — I will arise and shine.

 **ANCHOR** — Isaiah 60:1-3 (NIV) — "Arise, shine, for your light has come, and the glory of the Lord 'rises upon you.' See, darkness covers the earth and thick darkness is over the peoples, but the Lord rises upon you and His glory appears over you. Nations will come to your light, and kings to the brightness of your dawn."

Revelation 21:23-24 (NLT) — "And the city has no need of sun or moon, for the glory of God illuminates the city, and the Lamb is its light. The nations will walk in its light, and the kings of the world will enter the city in all their glory."

As a reformer created for impact, you are ready to take the revelation and understanding from your study of the Seven Mountains to arise and shine. You are ready to be the fulfillment of Isaiah 60:1-3, shining your light and making God known in the world around you. Consider the following prompts to help you further assimilate this charge.

1. Discuss how you will take what you have learned about the Seven Mountains to help you discover God's purpose for your life.

2. Think of a time when you may have believed the lie that your life doesn't matter. How would you encourage someone else that may be experiencing the same thing and help them believe the truth that their life does matter?

DAY 2
ALL THE CHILDREN OF THE WORLD

You understand the significance of being present for the person God puts in front of you.

I will love others as Christ has loved me.

Isaiah 41:10 (NKJV) — "Fear not, for I *am* with you; Be not dismayed, for I *am* your God. I will strengthen you, Yes, I will help you, I will uphold you with My righteous right hand."

John 3:16 (NKJV) — "For God so loved the world that He gave His only begotten Son, that whoever believes in Him should not perish but have everlasting life."

Journeying together, we ask God for the grace and capacity to be more like Him, present for the one, transcending cultures and ideologies. Why? Because Jesus loves all the children, all the children of the world. Reflect on the following prompts as you engage Heaven for your spiritual expansion.

1. **Compare what it means to be an orphan to what it feels like to know that you are a child of God.**

2. **Share challenges or biases you might have, or witnessed others having, regarding different cultures or ethnicities and ways we can practice seeing all God's children the way He sees them.**

DAY 3
OAKS OF RIGHTEOUSNESS

You understand the honor of the role that you have been called to in establishing the Kingdom of God.

I will partner with God to rebuild the ancient ruins.

Isaiah 61:1-4 (NIV) — "The Spirit of the Sovereign Lord is on me, because the Lord has anointed me to proclaim good news to the poor. He has sent me to bind up the brokenhearted, to proclaim freedom for the captives and release from darkness for the prisoners, to proclaim the year of the Lord's favor

and the day of vengeance of our God, to comfort all who mourn, and provide for those who grieve in Zion—to bestow on them a crown of beauty instead of ashes, the oil of joy instead of mourning, and a garment of praise instead of a spirit of despair. They will be called oaks of righteousness, a planting of the Lord for the display of his splendor. They will rebuild the ancient ruins and restore the places long devastated; they will renew the ruined cities that have been devastated for generations."

Revelation 22:1-2 (NLT) — "Then the angel showed me a river with the water of life, clear as crystal, flowing from the throne of God and of the Lamb. It flowed down the center of the main street. On each side of the river grew a tree of life, bearing twelve crops of fruit, with a fresh crop each month. The leaves were used for medicine to heal the nations."

Wow! God calls you strong oaks of righteousness. He has chosen you to partner with in the rebuilding of ancient ruins and the restoration of devastated places. Strengthen yourself in the Lord by contemplating the following prompts.

1. Describe God's unconditional love, and how you can apply this idea in your relationships with others.

2. Discuss the idea of hidden agendas and how this relates to walking in authenticity.

DAY 4
MERCY REIGNS OVER JUDGMENT

You understand how judgment can operate as a roadblock to God working in your life and the life of others.

I will give the mercy to others that has been given to me.

James 2:13 (NLT) — "There will be no mercy for those who have not shown mercy to others. But if you have been merciful, God will be merciful when he judges you."

> **2 John 1:3** (NIV) — "Grace, mercy and peace from God the Father and from Jesus Christ, the Father's Son, will be with us in truth and love."

We have learned the importance of continually separating ourselves from a spirit of judgment—against ourselves and others. We choose mercy towards others because God first chose mercy toward us. Take time to journal your thoughts around the following prompts. Share with a friend.

1. Compare and contrast the relationships between showing mercy to others and receiving mercy from God.

2. Describe the role of the Holy Spirit when discerning the difference between conviction and guilt and shame.

DAY 5
PRAYER IS NOT ENOUGH

You understand that standing in the gap goes beyond praying and involves taking action.

I will stand in the gap.

James 2:17 (NLT) — "So you see, faith by itself isn't enough. Unless it produces good deeds, it is dead and useless."

Ezekiel 22:30 (NLT) — "I looked for someone who might rebuild the wall of righteousness that guards the land. I searched for someone to stand in the gap in the wall so I wouldn't have to destroy the land, but I found no one."

Think about it! You were created to stand in the gap with a solution to a problem in the world. Your prayers coupled together with your actions can bring what is needed to a particular situation and at just the right time. Ask God what He wants to show you in this area as you consider the following prompts.

1. List some ways you can use your creative abilities, intellect, and actions to intercede—stand in the gap—for your friends and their assignments and callings.

2. Reflecting on what you have learned, journal some of the ways you can stand against the enemy on the Seven Mountains.

DAY 6
GRACE, GRACE, GOD'S GRACE

You understand the grace that has been shown toward you and are able to reflect it back to others.

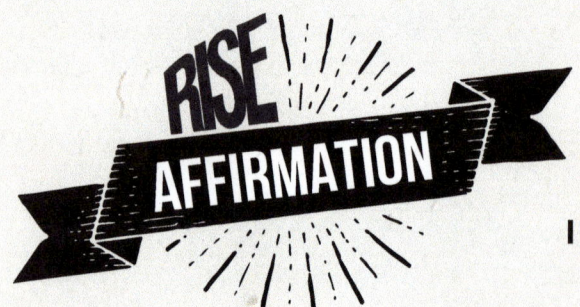

I will give grace to others.

Romans 11:6 (NLT) — "And since it is through God's kindness, then it is not by their good works. For in that case, God's grace would not be what it really is—free and undeserved."

Romans 5:2 (ESV) — "Through Him we have also obtained access by faith into this grace in which we stand, and we rejoice in hope of the glory of God."

Free and undeserved—His acceptance, His redemption, His wisdom, His provision, His joy, His good plans, and His power. Freely we have received, freely let us give. As you reflect on the prompts below, remember all the ways you have received grace from God.

1. Differentiate between religiosity and grace in how they approach addressing someone's sin and heart.

2. Write a blog on encouraging individuals to both receive God's grace and extend it to others as they journey through life and face various challenges.

DAY 7
FRIEND OF SINNERS

You understand you can be a friend of someone who doesn't believe the same way you do without jeopardizing your integrity.

I will avoid compromising alliances.

Exodus 34:12 (NLT) — "Be very careful never to make a treaty with the people who live in the land where you are going. If you do, you will follow their evil ways and be trapped."

Exodus 23:33 (NIV) — "Do not let them live in your land or they will cause you to sin against me, because the worship of their gods will certainly be a snare to you."

Demonstrating God's love involves intently listening to the Holy Spirit. As we consider being friends with those who may not believe the same way, we can ask the Holy Spirit for common ground, all while using discernment. We do this always mindful of maintaining integrity and avoiding alliances that may lead you astray. Take time to journal your thoughts around the prompts below.

1. Share an example from your own life where you were able to be a friend to someone without compromising your values or beliefs.

2. Discuss ways you can be a positive influencer and maintain your values without being negatively influenced by others.

DAY 8
CELEBRATE!

You understand the importance of not disregarding past works, but rather building on the accomplishments of others from history and previous generations.

I am a legacy builder in the Kingdom.

Hebrews 12:1 (NKJV) — "Therefore we also, since we are surrounded by so great a cloud of witnesses, let us lay aside every weight, and the sin which so easily ensnares *us*, and let us run with endurance the race that is set before us."

Psalms 112:1-3 (NIV) — "Praise the Lord. Blessed are those who fear the Lord, who find great delight in his commands. Their children will be mighty in the land; the generation of the upright will be blessed. Wealth and riches are in their houses, and their righteousness endures forever."

We recognize and affirm the positive contributions of all individuals, regardless of faith, when it aligns with the essence of establishing God's Kingdom in the Mountains of Culture. We ask Him to help foster our understanding and open hearts to Him, taking what we have learned from past generations, we move forward building on the lessons learned. Consider the following prompts as you explore building strategies with God.

1. List examples in history or modern day where someone contributed positively to society without necessarily realizing it aligns with God's kingdom values.

2. Describe the relationship between different generations and their role in society's progress.

DAY 9
PRISONERS OF HOPE

You understand the need to maintain hope in all situations.

I am a prisoner of hope.

Zechariah 9:12 (NKJV) — "Return to the stronghold, you prisoners of hope. Even today I declare that I will restore double to you."

Hebrews 6:19 (NLT) — "This hope is a strong and trustworthy anchor for our souls. It leads us through the curtain into God's inner sanctuary."

Hope is defined as the expectation of God's goodness, anchoring us in the belief that He redeems and restores all things. Despite adversity, we can maintain hope in every circumstance, knowing that God's timing and ways surpass our own. As reformers in society, our privilege lies in carrying hope for individuals, communities, and nations, trusting in the eventual fulfillment of God's Kingdom on Earth. Ask God what He wants to show you in this area as you consider the following prompts.

1. Describe ways young reformers, like yourself, carry hope for everyone, every situation, and every nation, as mentioned in the text? What practical steps can you take to do this.

2. Discuss the role hope plays in countering setbacks and disappointments.

DAY 10
GET UP AND SHOW UP!

UNDERSTANDING

You understand that God's promise and presence will empower you to fulfill your assignment.

AFFIRMATION

I will advance the Kingdom in my sphere of influence.

ANCHOR

Deuteronomy 31:8 (NLT) — "Do not be afraid or discouraged, for the LORD will personally go ahead of you. He will be with you; he will neither fail you nor abandon you."

Matthew 11:30 (NLT) — "For my yoke is easy to bear, and the burden I give you is light."

As we close, we are urged to action, reminding ourselves of our unique role in God's grand narrative of redemption and restoration on the Earth. While challenges may arise, the promise of God's presence and support empowers us to fulfill our purpose with confidence. We are committed to doing our part to usher in the Kingdom as God fulfills His promise of granting the nations for our inheritance. Reflect on the following prompts as you go forth.

1. Share what might be three next steps for exploring and determining which role they are called to play as a reformer on their respective mountain.

2. Explain the four primary roles shared for contributing to reformation and the Kingdom.

CONGRATULATIONS, YOU'VE REACHED THE FINAL PART OF YOUR JOURNEY THROUGH THE SEVEN MOUNTAINS OF CULTURE!

Consider the Seven Mountains of Culture you've learned about. Find someone in your family or community that has a role on a mountain that you're interested in. Consider asking them if you could interview them for the purpose of learning more about that area of culture, the challenges they face, the ways they are making a difference, and any other wisdom they would be willing to share with you. You can film the interview, record it, or take notes. Maybe they will even let you spend a day watching what they do and how they do it. Ask the Holy Spirit to use the time to speak to you about your own next steps towards your role in the Seven Mountains.